Curry Craze: Ultimate Guide to 100 Flavorful Recipes

De Saucy Sizzles

Copyright © 2023 De Saucy Sizzles
All rights reserved.
:

Contents

INTRODUCTION 7
1. Thai Green Curry 8
2. Indian Chicken Curry 9
3. Japanese Curry Rice 10
4. Malaysian Beef Rendang 11
5. Vietnamese Lemongrass Chicken Curry 12
6. Indonesian Nasi Goreng 13
7. Thai Massaman Curry 15
8. Korean Kimchi Stew 16
9. Singaporean Laksa 17
10. Thai Red Curry with Shrimp 18
11. Indian Lamb Curry 19
12. Malaysian Chicken Satay with Peanut Sauce 20
13. Burmese Chicken Curry 21
14. Sri Lankan Fish Curry 22
15. Thai Pineapple Curry 23
16. Vietnamese Pho 24
17. Indonesian Gado Gado 25
18. Thai Panang Curry 26
19. Japanese Katsu Curry 27
20. Korean Spicy Tofu Stew (Soonubu Jjigae) 28
21. Indian Butter Chicken 29
22. Malaysian Curry Laksa 31
23. Thai Yellow Curry 32
24. Indonesian Beef Rendang 33
25. Vietnamese Beef Pho 34
26. Thai Massaman Curry with Beef 35
27. Japanese Chicken Katsu Curry 36

28. Korean Bulgogi 37

29. Singaporean Hainanese Chicken Rice 38

30. Thai Tom Yum Soup 39

31. Indian Chana Masala 40

32. Malaysian Nasi Lemak 41

33. Vietnamese Caramelized Clay Pot Fish 42

34. Indonesian Sate Ayam (Chicken Satay) 43

35. Thai Coconut Curry Noodles (Khao Soi) 44

36. Japanese Miso Soup 46

37. Korean Japchae 46

38. Thai Red Curry with Tofu 48

39. Indian Vegetable Curry 49

40. Malaysian Roti Canai with Curry Sauce 50

41. Vietnamese Shrimp Curry 52

42. Indonesian Soto Ayam 53

43. Thai Green Curry with Fish 54

44. Japanese Curry Udon 55

45. Korean Dak Galbi (Spicy Stir-fried Chicken) 56

46. Singaporean Chili Crab 57

47. Thai Pad Thai 58

48. Indian Rogan Josh 59

49. Malaysian Mee Goreng 60

50. Vietnamese Lemongrass Beef Curry 61

51. Indonesian Beef Rendang with Coconut Rice 63

52. Thai Pumpkin Curry 64

53. Japanese Beef Curry 65

54. Korean Bibimbap 66

55. Singaporean Black Pepper Crab 67

56. Thai Tom Kha Gai (Coconut Chicken Soup) 68

57. Indian Palak Paneer..69
58. Malaysian Curry Puffs..70
59. Vietnamese Shaking Beef (Bo Luc Lac)..................................71
60. Indonesian Nasi Uduk..72
61. Thai Massaman Curry with Chicken.....................................73
62. Japanese Okonomiyaki..74
63. Korean Army Stew (Budae Jjigae)..75
64. Singaporean Fish Head Curry...76
65. Thai Red Curry with Vegetables...77
66. Indian Tandoori Chicken..79
67. Malaysian Prawn Noodles (Hokkien Mee)...........................80
68. Vietnamese Chicken Curry...81
69. Indonesian Beef Satay..82
70. Thai Pineapple Fried Rice...83
71. Japanese Miso Eggplant (Nasu Dengaku).............................84
72. Korean Spicy Seafood Stew (Jjamppong)..............................84
73. Singaporean Satay Bee Hoon..86
74. Thai Yellow Curry with Chicken..87
75. Indian Malai Kofta...88
76. Malaysian Curry Chicken Bun...89
77. Vietnamese Coconut Curry Chicken.....................................90
78. Indonesian Sayur Asem (Tamarind Vegetable Soup).........91
79. Thai Massaman Curry with Tofu...92
80. Japanese Yakisoba..93
81. Korean Jjajangmyeon...95
82. Singaporean Bak Kut Teh...96
83. Thai Green Curry with Beef...97
84. Indian Chicken Biryani..98
85. Malaysian Assam Laksa...99

86. Vietnamese Clay Pot Chicken 100
87. Indonesian Opor Ayam (Chicken in Coconut Milk) 101
88. Thai Red Curry with Pork 103
89. Japanese Teriyaki Chicken 104
90. Korean Gamjatang (Spicy Pork Bone Soup) 105
91. Singaporean Char Kway Teow 106
92. Thai Pad See Ew 107
93. Indian Egg Curry 108
94. Malaysian Curry Mee 109
95. Vietnamese Shrimp Pho 110
96. Indonesian Sambal Goreng Udang (Spicy Stir-fried Shrimp) 111
97. Thai Yellow Curry with Seafood 112
98. Japanese Tempura 113
99. Korean Doenjang Jjigae (Fermented Soybean Paste Stew) 114
100. Malaysian Beef Curry 115
CONCLUSION 117

INTRODUCTION

Welcome to Curry Craze: Your Ultimate Guide to 100 Flavorful Recipes. This cookbook is your gateway to a world of delicious and unique curries from around the globe. From mild to spicy, traditional to contemporary, Curry Craze has something for everyone.

Whether you're a novice in the kitchen or a seasoned cook, this cookbook provides you with easy-to-follow recipes that you can use to create flavorful curries. You'll find recipes for all the classics—दाल भाजी, चावलचटपटा, फ्राई चकिन, and वाली कुररी—in addition to some truly unique creations.

Learn how to whip up classic Indian-style curries like मसाला दाल and बैगन की सब्ज़ी. Venture into the world of Caribbean and African curries with dishes like Jamaican Curry Chicken and West African Peanut Stew. Whip up some Thai street food-style creations, like Spicy Coconut Chicken Curry and Curry Rice Noodle Salad. And explore the flavors of Persia with recipes like Khoresh-e Fesenjan and Mutton Curry.

As you explore the pages of Curry Craze, you'll learn about the unique ingredients used in many curries and discover a variety of techniques for layering and balancing flavor. Each recipe includes a full list of ingredients, step-by-step instructions, and an introduction that provides helpful tips—so you'll be able to take on any curry with confidence.

So grab your apron and get ready to explore the world of curry! With Curry Craze as your guide, you'll be able to create aromatic, flavor-packed dishes from India, Asia, Africa, and beyond. Enjoy!

1. Thai Green Curry

A fragrant and flavorful Thai green curry is a classic comfort food. This dish is made from a mixture of curry paste, coconut milk, and other Ingredients. The intense flavor and creamy texture of this delectable dish make it a favorite of Thai cuisine lovers around the world.

Serving: 4
Preparation Time: 10 mins
Ready Time: 25 mins

Ingredients:
- 3 tablespoons Thai green curry paste
- 1 can coconut milk
- 1 tablespoon fish sauce
- 1 ½ cups chicken broth/stock
- 1 ½ tablespoons brown sugar
- 2 tablespoons vegetable oil
- 2 cloves garlic, minced
- 1 large onion, diced
- 1 tablespoon freshly grated ginger
- 2 bell peppers, sliced
- 2 carrots, diced
- 1 pound chicken thighs, boneless and skinless
- 1 bunch of fresh basil
- 2 tablespoons lime juice

Instructions:
1. Heat the oil in a large pot over medium-high heat.
2. Add the garlic and onion and cook until the onion is soft and translucent.
3. Add the curry paste, coconut milk, fish sauce, chicken broth, and brown sugar and bring to a boil.
4. Reduce the heat and simmer for 10 minutes.
5. Add the bell peppers, carrots, and chicken and continue to simmer for another 10 minutes.
6. Add the basil and lime juice and cook for a final 5 minutes.
7. Serve over steamed rice or noodles.

Nutrition information:
Calories: 322, Total Fat: 19g, Saturated Fat: 13g, Cholesterol: 107mg, Sodium: 1015mg, Total Carbohydrate: 13g, Dietary Fiber: 3g, Protein: 24g

2. Indian Chicken Curry

Indian Chicken Curry is a flavorful and comforting dish made with marinated chicken simmered in a fragrant onion-tomato curry sauce. It's an easy Chicken Curry recipe made in the classic Indian style.
Serving: 4
Preparation time: 20 minutes.
Ready time: 40 minutes.

Ingredients:
- 2 lbs boneless, skinless chicken, cubed
- 2 tablespoons olive oil
- 2 tablespoons finely chopped garlic
- 1 tablespoons finely chopped ginger
- 2 medium onions, diced
- 2 bay leaves
- 1 teaspoon garam masala
- 2 teaspoons coriander powder
- 1 teaspoon cumin powder
- 2 teaspoons turmeric powder
- 1 teaspoon paprika
- 2 teaspoons Kashmiri chilli powder or regular chilli powder
- 1 large tomato, diced
- 2 cups chicken stock
- Salt to taste
- 2 tablespoons freshly chopped coriander leaves, for Serving:

Instructions:
1. In a large bowl, add the chicken cubes, 1 teaspoon of garam masala, 1 teaspoon of coriander powder, 1 teaspoon of cumin powder, 1 teaspoon of turmeric powder, 1 teaspoon of paprika and 1 teaspoon of Kashmiri chilli powder. Mix everything together and let it sit for 15 minutes.

2. Heat the olive oil in a large pot over medium heat. Add the garlic and ginger and cook for a few minutes, stirring often, until fragrant. Add the onions and bay leaves and cook for a few more minutes, until the onions become translucent.

3. Add the marinated chicken to the pot and cook for 5 minutes, stirring often. Add the tomato and cook for another 5 minutes, stirring often. Add the remaining spices and mix everything together.

4. Pour the chicken stock into the pot and bring the mixture to a boil. Reduce the heat to low and let it simmer for 20 minutes.

5. Check the curry for seasoning and add salt as needed. Cook for a few minutes more, until the chicken is cooked through.

6. Serve the Indian Chicken Curry with freshly chopped coriander leaves.

Nutrition information: Calories: 209, Total Fat: 5.5g, Sodium: 330mg, Carbohydrate: 6.1g, Protein: 30g

3. Japanese Curry Rice

Japanese Curry Rice is a popular Japanese dish made from a mixture of curry roux, vegetables and protein. It is a simple one-pan meal typically served over sticky, rice. It is easy to make and requires minimal Ingredients.

Serving: 4
Preparation time: 10 minutes
Ready time: 25 minutes

Ingredients:
- 1 tablespoons Olive Oil
- 2 tablespoons Curry Powder
- 1 Onion (diced)
- 1 Potato (diced)
- 1 Carrot (diced)
- 500 grams Ground Beef
- 4 cups White Rice (uncooked)
- 500 ml Water
- 1-2 tablespoons Curry Roux

Instructions:

1. Heat olive oil in a large skillet over medium heat.
2. Add in curry powder, and onion and saute for 3-4 minutes until the onions are translucent.
3. Add the potato, carrots, and ground beef to the skillet and cook for 8-10 minutes until the ground beef is cooked through.
4. Add the rice to the skillet and stir to combine.
5. Pour in the water and bring to a boil.
6. Reduce the heat to low-medium and simmer for 15 minutes, uncovered, until the ric is cooked.
7. Add the curry roux and stir until it melts and is evenly distributed.

Nutrition information :
- Calories : 617
- Total Fat: 14.5 g
- Saturated Fat: 4.1 g
- Cholesterol: 73 mg
- Sodium: 371 mg
- Total Carbohydrate: 78.7 g
- Dietary Fiber: 4.1 g
- Sugars: 2.5 g
- Protein: 33.2 g

4. Malaysian Beef Rendang

Malaysian Beef Rendang is a classic Malaysian curry dish consisting of tenderized beef cooked in a spicy coconut-based sauce. It is loved for its complex flavor and its sweet and spicy aroma.
Serving: 8
Preparation Time: 15 minutes
Ready Time: 2 hours

Ingredients:
- 2 tablespoons oil
- 2 pounds beef, cubed
- 2 tablespoons garlic, minced
- 2 tablespoons ginger, minced
- 2-3 lemongrass stalks, chopped
- 2 onions, diced

- 1 teaspoon ground cardamom
- 2 teaspoons ground coriander
- 1 teaspoon cumin powder
- 2 teaspoon turmeric powder
- 2 teaspoon paprika
- 1 tablespoon ground chilli powder
- 1 cup coconut milk
- Salt to taste
- 2 limes, juiced
- 2 tablespoons fresh cilantro, chopped

Instructions:
1. Heat the oil in a large pot over medium heat.
2. Add the cubed beef and cook for 3-4 minutes, stirring occasionally.
3. Add the garlic, ginger, lemongrass, and onions, and cook for 3-4 more minutes, or until the onions are softened and lightly browned.
4. Stir in the cardamom, coriander, cumin, turmeric, paprika and chilli powder until everything is coated with the spices.
5. Pour in the coconut milk and bring the mixture to a boil. Reduce the heat to medium-low and simmer, stirring occasionally, for 1-1.5 hours or until the beef is tender.
6. Season with salt and, if desired, add more chilli powder if you want it to be spicier.
7. Once the beef is cooked, stir in the lime juice and cilantro.
8. Serve over rice.

Nutrition information: (Per Serving)
Calories: 414 kcal, Carbohydrates: 5 g, Protein: 29 g, Fat: 28 g, Saturated Fat: 16 g, Cholesterol: 94 mg, Sodium: 172 mg, Potassium: 485 mg, Fiber: 1 g, Sugar: 2 g, Vitamin A: 350 IU, Vitamin C: 14 mg, Calcium: 18 mg, Iron: 2.5 mg

5. Vietnamese Lemongrass Chicken Curry

Vietnamese Lemongrass Chicken Curry is a flavorful dish that combines the traditional zest of lemongrass with mild spices. This is a group of delicious dishes that are sure to hit the spot!
Serving: 6

Preparation Time: 15 minutes
Ready Time: 1 hour

Ingredients:
-2 tablespoons vegetable oil
-1 pound boneless, skinless chicken thighs, cubed
-1 onion, diced
-2 cloves garlic, minced
-1-inch piece of fresh ginger, peeled and minced
-2 tablespoons red Thai curry paste
-1 stalk lemongrass, trimmed and minced
-1 (14-ounce) can coconut milk
-2 tablespoons fish sauce
-1 tablespoon light brown sugar
-1 red bell pepper, seeded and diced
-1/2 cup fresh cilantro, chopped

Instructions:
1. Heat oil in a large skillet over medium-high heat. Add chicken and cook, stirring occasionally, until golden brown, about 6 minutes.
2. Add onion and garlic; cook until onion is softened, about 3 minutes.
3. Stir in ginger, curry paste, lemongrass, and coconut milk. Bring to a simmer.
4. Reduce heat to low and simmer until chicken is cooked through, about 20 minutes.
5. Stir in fish sauce, sugar, and bell pepper; cook until bell pepper is tender, about 5 minutes.
6. Stir in cilantro. Serve over steamed jasmine rice.

Nutrition information: Calories: 439, Fat: 27g, Saturated Fat: 16g, Cholesterol: 103mg, Sodium: 566mg, Potassium: 481mg, Carbohydrates: 18g, Fiber: 3g, Sugar: 7g, Protein: 30g, Vitamin A: 1690 IU, Vitamin C: 26.5mg, Calcium: 68mg, Iron: 3.2mg

6. Indonesian Nasi Goreng

Indonesian Nasi Goreng is a traditional Indonesian dish which is a fried rice dish with added vegetables and proteins. It is full of flavor and comfort food.

Serving: 4
Preparation Time: 15 minutes
Ready Time: 20 minutes

Ingredients:
- 4 cups of cooked long grain rice
- 2 tablespoons of vegetable oil
- 2 eggs, lightly beaten
- 2 cloves of garlic, minced
- 2 shallots, chopped
- 2 large red chilies, chopped
- 2 cups of vegetables, diced
- 4 tablespoons of sweet soy sauce
- 2 tablespoons of fish sauce
- 2 tablespoons of kecap manis, sweet Indonesian soy sauce
- Optional proteins, such as chicken, tofu, shrimp, beef, etc.

Instructions:
1. Heat the vegetable oil in a wok or large skillet over medium-high heat.
2. Once the oil is hot, add the eggs and scramble until cooked through.
3. Add the garlic, shallots, chilies, and vegetables and cook for about 5 minutes.
4. Add the cooked rice to the wok and toss to combine.
5. Add the sweet soy sauce, fish sauce, and kecap manis and toss to combine.
6. Add the optional proteins and cook until they are cooked through.
7. Serve hot with some chopped green onion and lime wedges.

Nutrition information:
Serving Size - 1 cup
Calories - 250 kcal
Total Fat - 8g
Saturated Fat - 1g
Cholesterol - 92mg
Sodium - 992mg
Potassium - 101mg
Total Carbohydrate - 33g

Dietary Fiber - 2g
Sugar - 3g
Protein - 9g

7. Thai Massaman Curry

Thai Massaman Curry is a rich, creamy, and mildly spicy curry dish, originating from Thailand. It typically features potatoes, peanuts, and other vegetables, cooked in a fragrant coconut-based curry sauce.
Serving: This dish yields 8 servings.
Preparation time:
This dish requires 15 minutes of preparation time.
Ready time: This dish requires 45 minutes to be ready.

Ingredients:
- 2 tablespoons of vegetable oil or coconut oil
- 2 medium onions (chopped)
- 1 (13.5 ounc) can of coconut milk
- 2 tablespoons of Massaman curry paste
- 2 potatoes (diced)
- 2 carrots (diced)
- 1/2 cup of peanuts
- 2 tablespoons of soy sauce
- 1 lime (quartered)
- 2 tablespoons of brown sugar
- 1/4 cup of cilantro (for garnish)

Instructions:
1. Heat the vegetable or coconut oil in a large saucepan over medium heat. Once hot, add the chopped onions and cook until softened, about 5 minutes.
2. Pour in the coconut milk and Massaman curry paste, stirring to combine.
3. Add the potatoes and carrots to the pan and bring to a boil. Reduce heat to a low simmer and let cook until the potatoes and carrots are tender, about 15 minutes.

4. Once finished, stir in the peanuts, soy sauce, lime juice, and brown sugar. Continue to cook until everything is heated through, about 5 minutes more.
5. Garnish with freshly chopped cilantro and serve.

Nutrition information:
Per serving this dish yields 187 calories, 13.4g fat, 5.3g carbohydrates, and 2.5g protein.

8. Korean Kimchi Stew

Korean Kimchi Stew is a spicy, savory dish that combines the fermented veggie kimchi with a beef and pork broth. It's a flavorful meal that's easy to make and even easier to enjoy.
Serving: 4
Preparation time: 10 mins
Ready time: 30 mins

Ingredients:
- Kimchi, 2 cups
- Ground beef or pork, 1/3 cup
- Garlic, 2 cloves (minced)
- Onion, 1/4 cup (diced)
- Gochugaru (red pepper flakes), 1 teaspoon
- Gochujang (red pepper paste), 1 tablespoon
- Soy Sauce, 1 tablespoon
- Cooking oil, 2 tablespoons
- Water, 4-5 cups

Instructions:
1. Preheat the cooking oil in a saucepan over medium heat.
2. Once the oil is hot, add the onion and garlic and cook for 2-3 minutes until softened.
3. Add the ground beef or pork and cook for another 3-4 minutes.
4. Add the kimchi, gochugaru, gochujang, and soy sauce and cook for an additional 2-3 minutes.
5. Pour in the water and bring the stew to a boil.

6. Reduce the heat and simmer for 10-15 minutes until the flavors have melded together.
7. Serve the stew with steamed rice and enjoy.

Nutrition information: Calories: 253 kcal, Carbohydrates: 14 g, Protein: 14 g, Fat: 16 g, Saturated Fat: 5 g, Cholesterol: 40 mg, Sodium: 880 mg, Potassium: 313 mg, Fiber: 1 g, Sugar: 4 g, Vitamin A: 184 IU, Vitamin C: 0.7 mg, Calcium: 22 mg, Iron: 1.3 mg

9. Singaporean Laksa

Singaporean Laksa is an aromatic and rich soup that packs tons of flavor. It is a perfect recipe to try when you crave for some Asian flavors.
Serving: 4
Preparation Time: 10 minutes
Ready Time: 25 minutes

Ingredients:
- 2 tablespoons vegetable oil
- 2 cloves garlic, minced
- 2-inch piece fresh ginger, grated
- 2 shallots, diced
- 2 tablespoons laksa paste, or to taste
- 2 cups chicken broth
- 1 tablespoon fish sauce
- 2 teaspoons brown sugar
- 1 (14 ounce) can coconut milk
- 10 ounces cooked shrimp, diced
- 1 red bell pepper, diced
- 1/2 head bok choy, halved lengthwise
- 1/2 cup cooked thin rice vermicelli noodles
- 2 tablespoons fresh cilantro, minced
- Lime wedges, for garnish

Instructions:
1. Heat the vegetable oil in a large pot over medium-high heat.
2. Add the garlic, ginger, and shallots to the pot and cook until softened, about 5 minutes.

3. Add the laksa paste and cook for 1 minute.
4. Stir in the chicken broth, fish sauce, and brown sugar. Bring to a boil, reduce the heat to a simmer and cook for 10 minutes.
5. Add the coconut milk, shrimp, red pepper, and bok choy. Simmer for 5 minutes.
6. Add the noodles and cilantro and stir to combine.
7. Taste and adjust seasoning with salt and pepper, if desired.
8. Ladle into bowls and garnish with lime wedges.

Nutrition information: Calories: 250, Fat: 15 g, Carbohydrates: 19 g, Protein: 15 g, Sodium: 980 mg

10. Thai Red Curry with Shrimp

Thai red curry with shrimp is a delicious and fragrant dish with traditional Thai flavors. It's easy to make and boasts bold flavors of red curry paste and a creamy coconut milk base. It's sure to be a hit with friends and family alike.

Serving: 4
Preparation Time: 10 minutes
Ready Time: 25 minutes

Ingredients:
- 2 tablespoons vegetable oil
- 2 tablespoons Thai red curry paste
- 1 can (14 ounces) coconut milk
- 4 kaffir lime leaves
- 1 large red bell pepper, diced
- 1 large onion, diced
- 1 cup sugar snap peas, trimmed
- 1 lb. medium shrimp, peeled and deveined
- 2 tablespoons fish sauce
- 2 tablespoons fresh lime juice
- 1 tablespoon fresh Thai basil, minced
- Salt and pepper to taste

Instructions:
1. In a large skillet or wok, heat vegetable oil over medium-high heat.

2. Add red curry paste and cook for about 1 minute, stirring constantly.
3. Pour in coconut milk and bring to a simmer.
4. Add kaffir lime leaves, red bell pepper, and onion and simmer for 5 minutes.
5. Add the sugar snap peas and shrimp and cook for an additional 5 minutes.
6. Add the fish sauce, lime juice, and Thai basil, stir to combine.
7. Taste and season with salt and pepper, to taste.
8. Serve hot over hot steamed jasmine or basmati rice.

Nutrition information: Per serving: Calories 370, Protein 26 g, Fat 20 g, Carbohydrates 17 g, Sodium 650 mg, Fiber 4 g

11. Indian Lamb Curry

This fragrant Indian Lamb Curry dish is sure to become a favorite in your home. It marries warm, comforting flavors in an easy-to-make dish.
Serving: 6-8
Preparation Time: 10 minutes
Ready Time: 40 minutes

Ingredients:
- 2 tablespoons cooking oil
- 2 large onions diced
- 2 cloves garlic minced
- 1 tablespoon grated ginger
- 1 teaspoon ground cumin
- 1 teaspoon garam masala
- 1 teaspoon ground coriander
- 1/2 teaspoon turmeric
- 2 to 3 tablespoons of curry powder
- 2-3 bay leaves
- 3 pounds of boneless lamb shoulder cut into 1 1/2-inch cubes
- 2 cans of coconut milk
- 1/2 cup of tomato paste
- Salt to taste
- 2 tablespoons fresh chopped cilantro

Instructions:
1. Heat the oil in a large pot over medium-high heat. Add the onion and cook until softened, about 5 minutes.
2. Add the garlic and ginger and cook for an additional minute.
3. Add the cumin, garam masala, coriander, turmeric, and curry powder and cook for 2 minutes, stirring constantly.
4. Add the bay leaves and the cubed lamb and stir to coat the lamb with the spices. Cook for an additional 5 minutes.
5. Pour in the coconut milk and tomato paste and turn the heat down to low.
6. Simmer for 25-30 minutes, stirring occasionally.
7. Add more salt to taste, if desired.
8. Garnish with fresh cilantro.

Nutrition information:
Calories: 569
Fat: 34g
Carbohydrates: 16g
Protein: 44g

12. Malaysian Chicken Satay with Peanut Sauce

Malaysian Chicken Satay with Peanut Sauce is a popular dish that's a hit amongst satay lovers. Marinated chicken is barbecued and served with a delicious, nutty peanut sauce that is irresistible.
Serving: 4
Preparation time: 15 minutes
Ready time: 1 hour

Ingredients:
- 500g chicken thigh fillets, trimmed and cut into 3cm pieces
- 2 tablespoons Malaysian curry powder
- ¼ cup vegetable oil
- ¼ cup white vinegar
- 2 teaspoons sugar
- 2 teaspoons fish sauce
- 2 cloves garlic, crushed

Instructions:
1. Place chicken into a large bowl and add curry powder, oil, vinegar, sugar, fish sauce and garlic. Stir until chicken is evenly coated. Cover and chill for 1 hour.
2. Remove from fridge and thread chicken onto skewers.
3. Preheat barbecue or griddle pan to medium heat and cook chicken skewers, turning until cooked through – about 8 minutes.
4. Serve hot accompanied with peanut sauce for dipping.

Nutrition information: Per serving: Calories 359, Protein 28g, Fat 18g, Carbs 15g, Sugar 5g.

13. Burmese Chicken Curry

Burmese Chicken Curry is a traditional dish from Burma which is made with a smooth and creamy yellow curry sauce and tender pieces of chicken. It has a unique flavor from the combination of lemon, ginger, cilantro, and turmeric.
Serving: 6
Preparation time: 30 minutes
Ready time: 2 hours

Ingredients:
2 tablespoons vegetable oil
1-2 onions, finely chopped
4 cloves garlic, minced
2 tablespoons fresh ginger, minced
2 tablespoons ground cumin
1 teaspoon ground turmeric
1 teaspoon ground cinnamon
1/4 teaspoon cayenne pepper
1 tablespoon lemon zest
2 lbs boneless chicken thighs, cut into small pieces
1/2 cup coconut milk
2 tablespoons fresh cilantro, chopped
Salt and pepper to taste

Instructions:

1. Heat the oil in a large saucepan over medium heat.
2. Add the onions and cook until they start to soften, about 5 minutes. Add the garlic, ginger, cumin, turmeric, cinnamon, cayenne pepper, and lemon zest and continue to cook for another 1-2 minutes.
3. Add the chicken and stir to combine with the spices. Cook for another 5 minutes, stirring often, until the chicken is browned.
4. Pour in the coconut milk and bring to a simmer. Reduce the heat to low and simmer for 45 minutes, stirring occasionally.
5. Add the cilantro and season to taste with salt and pepper.
6. Serve hot over steamed rice.

Nutrition information: Calories: 257kcal, Fat: 15.8g, Saturated Fat: 7.6g, Cholesterol: 92mg, Sodium: 116mg, Carbohydrates: 5.6g, Fiber: 1.4g, Protein: 22.3g

14. Sri Lankan Fish Curry

Sri Lankan Fish Curry is a classic dish made with flavorful spices and fragrant aromas. It is a combination of abundant red chilly, curry leaves smell of cumin seeds, and the sourness of tamarind combined with the flavour of fresh fish for a flavorful, spicy and comforting meal.
Serving: 6
Preparation time: 30 mins
Ready time: 1 hour

Ingredients:
- 2 tablespoons oil
- 1 teaspoon mustard seeds
- 2 onions (chopped)
- 4 cloves garlic (finely chopped)
- 2 tablespoons fish masala
- 2 teaspoons chili powder
- 2 teaspoons ground turmeric
- 2 tablespoons tamarind paste
- 1 cup coconut milk
- 2-3 cups water
- 2 pounds fish fillet (cut into cubes)
- 1-2 tablespoons fresh coriander (chopped for garnishing)

Instructions:
1. Heat oil in a large pan over medium-high heat.
2. Add mustard seeds to the oil and stir.
3. Add onions and garlic to the pan and cook until lightly browned.
4. Add fish masala, chili powder, and turmeric to the onions and mix.
5. Add tamarind paste, coconut milk, and water; mix together and bring to a boil.
6. Reduce heat to low and simmer for 10 minutes.
7. Add fish to the pan and cook for 10-15 minutes until cooked through.
8. Garnish with fresh coriander and serve.

Nutrition information: Per Serving: Calories: 263, Protein: 25.2g, Total Fat: 9.3g, Dietary Fiber: 4.2g, Total Carbohydrates: 24.5g

15. Thai Pineapple Curry

Thai Pineapple Curry is a classic Southeast Asian-style dish with a sweet and spicy flavor. This vegan-friendly dish combines the flavors of red curry paste, coconut milk, and fresh vegetables, finishing it off with a hint of sweetness from the pineapple.
Serving: 4-6
Preparation Time: 10 minutes
Ready Time: 30-40 minutes

Ingredients:
- 2 tablespoons of red curry paste
- 1 tablespoon of coconut oil
- 1 can (14 oz) of coconut milk
- 1 teaspoon of sugar
- 1 stalk of lemongrass, chopped
- 1 red bell pepper cored and diced
- 1 large carrot, peeled and chopped
- 1 onion, diced
- 2 cloves of garlic, crushed
- 2 tablespoons of coconut flakes
- 1/2 cup of pineapple chunks
- 2 tablespoons of chopped fresh cilantro

- 1 tablespoon of fresh lime juice
- Salt and pepper to taste

Instructions:
1. Heat curry paste and coconut oil in a large saucepan over medium heat.
2. Once heated, add the coconut milk, sugar, lemongrass, bell pepper, carrot, onion, garlic,and coconut flakes. Bring to a light boil and let simmer for 10 minutes, stirring frequently.
3. Add in the pineapple chunks, cilantro, lime juice, and salt and pepper to taste. Turn off heat and let the curry sit for 10 minutes.
4. Serve over rice, garnished with additional cilantro if desired.

Nutrition information:
Calories: 299
Carbohydrates: 18g
Fiber: 5g
Protein: 3g
Fat: 24g
Sugar: 11g

16. Vietnamese Pho

Vietnamese Pho is a traditional Vietnamese soup that is made with homemade beef or chicken broth and served with a variety of vegetables and herbs. It is a hearty, comforting dish that can be enjoyed as a light meal or as a warming snack.
Serving: Serves 4
Preparation Time: 15 minutes
Ready Time: 45 minutes

Ingredients:
- 4 shallots, diced
- 2 cloves garlic, minced
- 1 thumb-sized piece of ginger, grated
- 2 tablespoons cooking oil
- 2 tablespoons fish sauce
- 5-6 cups of beef or chicken broth

- 1 pound of beef rib eye, thinly sliced
- 4 bundles of rice vermicelli noodles
- Toppings of choice: bean sprouts, Thai basil, sliced limes, sliced jalapenos, sliced red bell peppers, cilantro

Instructions:
1. Heat a large pot or Dutch oven over medium heat. Add the diced shallots, minced garlic, and grated ginger to the pot and cook until softened, about 5 minutes.
2. Add the cooking oil, fish sauce, and beef or chicken broth to the pot and bring to a gentle simmer.
3. Add the thinly sliced beef to the broth and let simmer for 15-20 minutes.
4. Meanwhile, bring a separate pot of water to a boil. Add the rice vermicelli noodles to the boiling water and cook for 8-10 minutes, or until al dente.
5. To serve, place the cooked noodles in individual bowls. Ladle the broth and beef into the bowls and finish with desired toppings.

Nutrition information: Calories 344 kcal, Protein 20.6 g, Fat 18.5 g, Carbohydrates 18.7 g, Fiber 0.9 g, Sugar 0.6 g, Sodium 919 mg

17. Indonesian Gado Gado

Gado Gado is a popular Indonesian salad made with boiled vegetables, topped with a savory peanut sauce. It is a great vegan and vegetarian dish, and can be easily customized to suit a wide variety of tastes and dietary requirements.
Serving: 4
Preparation time: 30 minutes
Ready time: 30 minutes

Ingredients:
- 2 cups cooked potatoes
- 2 cups cooked green beans
- 4 hard-boiled eggs
- 2 cups bean sprouts
- 1/2 cup peanuts, roughly chopped

- 1/2 cup fresh cilantro
- 2 cloves garlic, minced
- 2 tablespoons fresh lime juice
- 2 tablespoons soy sauce
- 2 tablespoons peanut butter
- 2 tablespoons sambal oelek
- 2 tablespoons coconut sugar
- 2 tablespoons vegetable oil

Instructions:
1. In a large bowl, combine potatoes, green beans, eggs, bean sprouts, peanuts, and cilantro.
2. In a separate bowl, whisk together garlic, lime juice, soy sauce, peanut butter, sambal oelek, coconut sugar, and vegetable oil to make the dressing.
3. Pour the dressing over the vegetables and toss lightly to combine.
4. Divide the Gado Gado onto 4 plates and serve.

Nutrition information:
Calories: 243.8kcal, Protein: 10.6g, Carbs: 24.5g, Fiber: 3.6g, Fat: 11.9g

18. Thai Panang Curry

Thai Panang Curry is a spicy and creamy red curry made with panang curry paste, coconut milk, and protein of your choice. It is a popular Thai dish bursting with the flavors of lemongrass, chilies, and kaffir lime leaves.
Serving: 4
Preparation Time: 20 minutes
Ready Time: 30 minutes

Ingredients:
- 2 tablespoons panang curry paste
- 2 tablespoons oil
- 1 onion, sliced
- 2 cups coconut milk
- 4-6 ounces protein (pork, beef, chicken, tofu, or other)
- 1-3 tablespoons fish sauce

- 1 tablespoon brown sugar
- 2 tablespoons peanut butter
- 1/4 cup fresh basil or Thai basil leaves
- 2 kaffir lime leaves, optional
- 1 teaspoon minced garlic
- 1 teaspoon minced ginger

Instructions:
1. Heat oil in a large skillet over medium heat.
2. Add onion and sauté until softened, about 4 minutes.
3. Stir in curry paste and cook for 1 minute.
4. Add coconut milk, protein, fish sauce, sugar, peanut butter, basil leaves, kaffir lime leaves, garlic, and ginger. Simmer for 10 minutes.
5. Taste and adjust flavors to your liking and serve.

Nutrition information:
Calories: 275 kcal, Carbohydrates: 22 g, Protein: 13 g, Fat: 16 g, Saturated Fat: 11 g, Cholesterol: 26 mg, Sodium: 851 mg, Potassium: 424 mg, Fiber: 4 g, Sugar: 8 g, Vitamin A: 124 IU, Vitamin C: 9 mg, Calcium: 44 mg, Iron: 2 mg

19. Japanese Katsu Curry

Japanese Katsu Curry is a popular and comforting curry dish usually served with rice. It is typically made with deep-fried pork cutlet, which is known as "Katsu" and a savory curry sauce.

Serving - 4
Preparation time - 10 minutes
Ready time - 20 minutes

Ingredients:
- 4 boneless pork chops
- 1 cup panko breadcrumbs
- 1/2 cup all-purpose flour
- 2 eggs lightly beaten
- 1/4 teaspoon salt
- 1 teaspoon garlic powder
- 2 tablespoons oil

- 2 tablespoons butter
- 2 tablespoons all-purpose flour
- 1 tablespoon curry powder
- 1 teaspoon garam masala
- 2 tablespoons soy sauce
- 2 cups chicken broth
- 1 cup cooked rice

Instructions:
1. Take the boneless pork chops and coat with panko breadcrumbs, flour, eggs and salt.
2. Heat the oil and butter in a large skillet over medium-high heat.
3. Place the pork chops in the hot oil and cook for 2 minutes on each side until golden brown.
4. Remove the pork chops from the skillet and set aside.
5. In the same skillet, add the garlic powder, flour, curry powder, garam masala, soy sauce, and chicken broth.
6. Cook for a few minutes until the sauce thickens.
7. Return the pork chops to the skillet and cook for an additional 3 minutes.
8. Serve the pork chops with cooked rice.

Nutrition information
- Calories: 315
- Total fat: 16g
- Saturated fat: 4.5g
- Cholesterol: 97mg
- Sodium: 843mg
- Carbohydrates: 17g
- Protein: 25g

20. Korean Spicy Tofu Stew (Soonubu Jjigae)

Korean Spicy Tofu Stew, or Soonubu Jjigae, is a hearty, warming stew made with tofu, vegetables, and a deliciously spicy gochujang-based sauce.
Serving: 4
Preparation time: 10 minutes

Ready time: 30 minutes

Ingredients:
- 8 ounces medium-firm tofu, drained and cubed
- 2 tablespoons cooking oil
- 2 cups mixed mushrooms (such as shiitake, oyster, and enoki)
- 2 cloves garlic, minced
- 1 teaspoon gochujang (Korean chili paste)
- 1 teaspoon gochugaru (Korean chili flakes)
- 2 to 3 tablespoons light soy sauce
- 2 to 3 tablespoons sugar
- 1 cup white or green cabbage, sliced
- 1/2 cup Korean leeks, sliced
- 2 cups water
- 2 teaspoons baking soda
- Optional toppings: sesame seeds, scallion, boiled egg

Instructions:
1. Heat a large pot over medium-high heat and add cooking oil.
2. Add mushrooms and garlic and stir-fry for a few minutes.
3. Add gochujang, gochugaru, soy sauce, and sugar and cook for 1 to 2 minutes.
4. Add cabbage, Korean leeks, and cubed tofu.
5. Add the water and baking soda.
6. Lower the heat and simmer for 20 minutes.
7. Serve hot with optional toppings.

Nutrition information: (per servings) Calories: 210; Fat: 11g; Saturated Fat: 1.5g; Cholesterol: 0mg; Sodium: 510mg; Carbohydrates: 19g; Fiber: 4g; Sugar: 9g; Protein: 11g.

21. Indian Butter Chicken

Indian Butter Chicken is one of the most popular North Indian dishes. It is a savory and creamy dish composed of marinated chicken chunks slow-cooked with an irresistible spiced tomato cream sauce.
Serving: 4
Preparation Time: 15 mins

Ready Time: 30 mins

Ingredients:
- 4 chicken breasts, cut in cubes
- 2 tablespoons of olive oil
- 2 tablespoons of butter
- 2 onions, finely chopped
- 4 cloves of garlic, crushed
- 2 tablespoons of freshly grated ginger
- 1 teaspoon of ground cumin
- 1 teaspoon of ground coriander
- 1 teaspoon of garam masala
- 1 teaspoon of paprika
- 2 cups of tomato puree
- 1/2 cup of heavy cream
- Salt and pepper to taste

Instructions:
1. In a medium-sized bowl, mix together the cubed chicken, olive oil, salt, and pepper. Set aside.
2. Heat butter in a large skillet over medium heat. Add the onions and garlic, and sauté until the onions are softened, about 5 minutes.
3. Add the ginger, cumin, coriander, garam masala, and paprika. Stir and cook for another minute.
4. Add the tomato puree and bring to a boil. Reduce heat and simmer for 10 minutes, stirring often.
5. Add the marinated chicken cubes and cook for about 10 minutes, stirring occasionally.
6. Stir in the heavy cream and season with salt and pepper. Simmer for another 5 minutes.
7. Serve with rice or naan and enjoy!

Nutrition information:
Calories: 455kcal, Fat: 30g, Saturated Fat: 14g, Cholesterol: 103mg, Sodium: 427mg, Potassium: 849mg, Carbohydrates: 21g, Fiber: 3g, Sugar: 9g, Protein: 29g, Vitamin A: 970IU, Vitamin C: 13mg, Calcium: 85mg, Iron: 2mg

22. Malaysian Curry Laksa

Malaysian Curry Laksa is a flavorful noodle soup that combines a sweet and spicy coconut curry broth with rice noodles, tofu and vegetables.
Serving: 8
Preparation time: 10 minutes
Ready time: 30 minutes

Ingredients:
- 2 tablespoons vegetable oil
- 2 cloves garlic, finely chopped
- 2 tablespoons red curry paste
- 1 teaspoon ground turmeric
- 1 (14-ounce) can coconut milk
- 2 cups vegetable broth
- 1 (14-ounce) block of extra-firm tofu, pressed and cut into cubes
- 1 (8-ounce) package rice stick noodles
- 1/2 cup chopped green onions
- 2 cups fresh bean sprouts
- 2 teaspoon brown sugar
- Juice of 1 lime

Instructions:
1. Heat oil in a medium-large pot over medium heat. Add garlic and curry paste and stir-fry for about 1 minute.
2. Add turmeric and cook for 1 more minute.
3. Add coconut milk and vegetable broth and stir to combine.
4. Add tofu cubes and let simmer for 10 minutes.
5. Add the noodles, green onions, bean sprouts and sugar to the pot. Let cook for another 10-15 minutes.
6. When noodles are tender, turn off heat and add lime juice.
7. Serve hot with fresh chopped scallions on top.

Nutrition information: Per serving (1/8 of the entire recipe):
Calories: 253, Total Fat: 14g, Saturated Fat: 8g, Cholesterol: 0mg, Sodium: 302mg, Carbohydrates: 25g, Dietary Fiber: 2g, Sugars: 4g, Protein: 7g

23. Thai Yellow Curry

Thai Yellow Curry is an exquisite and classic Thai dish featuring a flavorful and creamy coconut milk base with an array of spices. It has a mild to medium heat and a delicious hint of sweetness from its sweet peppers.

Serving: 4
Preparation time: 10 minutes
Ready time: 20 minutes

Ingredients:
- 2 tablespoons vegetable oil
- 2 tablespoons freshly ground yellow curry paste
- 1 can (14.5-ounces) full-fat coconut milk
- ½ cup sliced onion
- 1 red bell pepper, diced
- 2 tablespoons fish sauce
- 2 tablespoons honey
- Juice of 1 lime
- 2 cups cooked chicken or shrimp
- 1 can (15-ounces) baby corn
- Handful of fresh basil, chopped

Instructions:
1. Heat the oil in a large skillet or wok over medium heat.
2. Add the curry paste and cook for a minute, stirring constantly.
3. Add the coconut milk and stir to combine.
4. Add the onion, bell pepper, fish sauce, honey, and lime juice.
5. Simmer for 5 minutes over low heat, stirring occasionally.
6. Add the chicken or shrimp and baby corn, simmer for a few minutes, until the chicken or shrimp is cooked through.
7. Taste and adjust seasonings, if needed.
8. Serve over steamed rice or noodles, garnished with the chopped basil.

Nutrition information: Per serving: Calories: 517, Fat: 33 g, Sodium: 742 mg, Carbohydrates: 33 g, Fiber: 6 g, Protein: 23 g

24. Indonesian Beef Rendang

Indonesian Beef Rendang is a delicious and incredibly flavorful beef stew with savory spices. This is a classic recipe that is sure to be a hit with everyone who tries it.

Serving: 8
Preparation Time: 20 minutes
Ready Time: 2 hours

Ingredients:
- 2 lbs. beef, cubed
- 3 cloves garlic, minced
- 1 large onion, chopped
- 2 inches ginger, minced
- 2 tablespoons veg oil
- 2 tablespoons coriander powder
- 2 tablespoons turmeric powder
- 2 tablespoons cumin powder
- 2 tablespoons tamarind paste
- 2 tablespoons palm sugar
- 2 - 3 red chilies, chopped
- 1-2 cups (240-480ml) coconut milk
- Salt to taste

Instructions:
1. Heat the oil in a large pot over medium heat and add the diced beef. Sear the beef for 5 minutes.
2. Add the garlic, onion, ginger, coriander powder, turmeric powder, cumin powder, tamarind paste, palm sugar, and red chilies to the pot, stirring to combine.
3. Reduce the heat to low and simmer for an hour, stirring occasionally.
4. Pour in the coconut milk and stir to combine. Simmer for 30-45 minutes, stirring occasionally, until the beef is tender and the sauce has thickened.
5. Season with salt to taste and serve.

Nutrition information: (per serving)
Calories: 286 kcal, Protein: 23.5 g, Carbohydrates: 8.6 g, Fiber: 2.2 g, Sugar: 3.8 g, Fat: 17.2 g, Cholesterol: 63 mg, Sodium: 17 mg.

25. Vietnamese Beef Pho

Vietnamese Beef Pho is a delicious and comforting noodle soup that features thinly sliced beef, herbs, and spices.
Serving: 2
Preparation Time: 15 minutes
Ready Time: 45 minutes

Ingredients:
- 2 cups beef broth
- 2 cups water
- 2 tablespoons fish sauce
- 2 tablespoons soy sauce
- 2 tablespoons brown sugar
- 1 cinnamon stick
- 1 star anise
- 2 cloves garlic, crushed
- 2-inch piece of fresh ginger, peeled and grated
- 1 teaspoon coriander seeds
- 2 teaspoons black peppercorns
- 2 tablespoons vegetable oil
- ¼ pound thinly sliced beef
- 4 ounces vermicelli or rice noodles
- ½ cup fresh bean sprouts
- 2 tablespoons chopped fresh cilantro
- 1 lime, cut into wedges
- Sliced jalapeno, for garnish (optional)

Instructions:
1. In a large saucepan, combine the beef broth, water, fish sauce, soy sauce, brown sugar, cinnamon stick, star anise, garlic, ginger, coriander seeds, and peppercorns. Bring to a boil, reduce to a simmer, and simmer for 25 minutes.
2. Strain the broth into a clean pot, discarding the solids. Return the broth to a simmer.
3. In a separate pan, heat the vegetable oil over medium-high heat. Add the beef and cook for 4-5 minutes, stirring occasionally, until lightly browned.

4. To serve, add the rice noodles or vermicelli to the simmering broth and cook until softened, about 2 minutes. Divide the noodles between two bowls.
5. Divide the cooked beef between the bowls, pouring any remaining cooking juices over the beef.
6. Top with bean sprouts, cilantro, and a squeeze of lime juice. Serve with sliced jalapenos, if desired.

Nutrition information: Per serving, this Vietnamese Beef Pho contains approx. 421 calories, 16.1g fat, 33.7g carbohydrates, 22.3g protein, and 7.6g fiber.

26. Thai Massaman Curry with Beef

Thai Massaman Curry with Beef is a traditional Thai curry with fall-apart tender beef simmered in a rich and creamy coconut based gravy. Fragrant spices and herbs like turmeric, cinnamon, and nutmeg add layers of flavor and aroma to this hearty comfort food.
Serving: 4-6
Preparation time: 15 minutes
Ready time: 45-50 minutes

Ingredients:
- 2 lbs stew meat, cut into cubes
- 2-3 tablespoon vegetable oil
- 3-4 tablespoons Massaman curry paste
- 2-3 tablespoons fish sauce
- 2 tablespoons tamarind paste
- 1 tablespoon brown sugar
- 1 (14.5-ounce) can coconut milk
- 2 potatoes, cut into 1-inch cubes
- 1/2 cup roasted peanuts
- Salt and pepper to taste
- Fresh cilantro to garnish

Instructions:
1. Heat oil in a large skillet over medium-high heat.

2. Add beef cubes and curry paste and stir fry for a few minutes until lightly browned.
3. Add fish sauce, tamarind paste, brown sugar, and coconut milk.
4. Bring to a simmer and cook, stirring occasionally, for 25-30 minutes until the beef is cooked through and the sauce thickens.
5. Add potatoes, peanuts, and salt and pepper to taste.
6. Cook an additional 10-15 minutes until potatoes are tender.
7. Serve with hot steamed rice and garnish with fresh cilantro.

Nutrition information: Per serving - Calories: 501; Total Fat: 28.6g; Saturated Fat: 17.1g; Protein: 25.2g; Carbohydrates: 39.2g; Fiber: 8.3g; Sugars: 6.5g; Sodium: 744mg

27. Japanese Chicken Katsu Curry

Japanese Chicken Katsu Curry is a savory dish of deep fried breaded chicken in a mild curry sauce. It is a popular home cooking dish in Japan and is also widely available in restaurants.
Serving: 4
Preparation time: 10 minutes
Ready time: 30-40 minutes

Ingredients:
- ½ cup All-purpose flour
- 1 teaspoon each garlic powder, onion powder and paprika
- 1 teaspoon black pepper
- 2 eggs
- 2-3 cups Panko breadcrumbs
- 4 chicken breasts
- 4 tablespoons unsalted butter
- 2 tablespoons all-purpose flour
- 1 teaspoon mild curry powder
- 1 onion, chopped
- 3 cloves garlic, minced
- 1 teaspoon grated fresh ginger
- 3 tablespoons tomato paste
- 1 teaspoon light brown sugar
- 1 teaspoon apple cider vinegar

- 2¼ cups chicken broth
- 2 tablespoons soy sauce
- 1 tablespoon cornstarch
- ½ teaspoon salt
- 2 tablespoons water

Instructions:
1. Preheat the oven to 350 degrees F (175 degrees C).
2. In a shallow dish, mix the flour, garlic powder, onion powder, and paprika.
3. In another shallow dish, beat the eggs.
4. Dip the chicken breasts in the egg mixture and then coat in the flour mixture.
5. Place the chicken breasts on a baking sheet and bake in the preheated oven for 25-30 minutes, or until cooked through.
6. In a large skillet, melt the butter over medium heat.
7. Add the flour and curry powder, and cook, stirring constantly, for 1-2 minutes.
8. Add the onion, garlic, and ginger and cook, stirring constantly, for 2-3 minutes, or until the onion has softened.
9. Add the tomato paste, brown sugar, and apple cider vinegar, and cook, stirring constantly, for 1 minute.
10. Add the chicken broth and bring to a boil.
11. Reduce the heat to low and stir in the soy sauce.
12. In a small bowl, mix the cornstarch and water until dissolved.
13. Add the cornstarch mixture to the skillet and stir until thickened.
14. Add the chicken breasts to the skillet and simmer for 10 minutes.

Nutrition information: Calories: 450; Fat: 8 g; Carbs: 51 g; Protein: 32 g

28. Korean Bulgogi

Korean Bulgogi is a classic Korean dish made of thinly sliced beef that is marinated in a flavorful and savory sauce. It can be cooked in a pan or over a barbecue and is usually served with rice or lettuce wraps.
Serving: 6
Preparation time: 20 minutes

Ready time: 15 minutes

Ingredients:
- 1 ½ lbs of thinly sliced sirloin, ribeye or chuck beef
- 2 tablespoons of sesame oil
- 2 tablespoons of soy sauce
- 2 tablespoons of mirin
- 2 tablespoons of brown sugar
- 2 cloves of minced garlic
- 2 teaspoons of grated ginger
- 1 teaspoon of black pepper

Instructions:
1. In a bowl, combine sesame oil, soy sauce, mirin, brown sugar, garlic, ginger, and black pepper.
2. Place the beef into a shallow dish and pour the marinade over the beef.
3. Allow the beef to marinade for 1-2 hours.
4. Heat a skillet or a barbecue over medium-high heat.
5. Add the beef to the skillet and cook for 3-4 minutes on each side until it is cooked through.
6. Serve the beef with rice or lettuce wraps.

Nutrition information: Per serving: 282 calories; 13.6g fat; 2.3g saturated fat; 31.6g protein; 10.3g carbohydrates; 1.7g sugar; 0g fiber; 536mg sodium.

29. Singaporean Hainanese Chicken Rice

Singaporean Hainanese Chicken Rice is a fragrant, flavorful, and comforting dish. It is a popular dish in many Asian countries and is often served as part of a larger meal. This dish is cooked with plenty of fragrant ginger, garlic, and pandan leaves as well as a unique blend of spices and seasonings.

Serving: 4-6
Preparation Time: 20 mins
Ready Time: 55 mins

Ingredients:
- 4-6 chicken breasts
- 4 cups of white rice
- 4 cloves garlic, minced
- 4 slices of ginger, minced
- 4 pandam leaves, finely chopped
- 2 TBSP of neutral oil
- 2 TBSP of light soy sauce
- 2 TBSP of sesame oil
- 2 TBSP of white vinegar
- 1 TBSP of sugar
- Salt and black pepper to taste

Instructions:
1. Heat a large non-stick pan over medium heat. Add oil, garlic, ginger, and pandam leaves. Cook until fragrant, about 2 minutes.
2. Add chicken breasts to pan and cook until lightly browned and cooked through, about 10 minutes.
3. Meanwhile, rinse and drain rice. Add rice to a medium pot. Pour 4 cups of water over the rice and bring to a boil. Reduce to low heat and simmer for 15 minutes.
4. During the final 5 minutes of cooking the rice, add the soy sauce, sesame oil, vinegar, and sugar. Stir to combine.
5. When rice is cooked, turn off heat and let stand for 5 minutes.
6. Serve chicken and rice together with a sprinkle of salt and black pepper.

Nutrition information:
Calories: 646 kcal, Carbs: 53 g, Protein: 37 g, Fat: 25 g, Sodium: 673 mg, Sugar: 3 g

30. Thai Tom Yum Soup

Thai Tom Yum Soup is a classic Southeast Asian soup with a spicy, sour, and savory broth that's full of flavorful Ingredients. It's a delicious, quick, and easy meal that's sure to please the whole family.
Serving: 4-6
Preparation time: 10 minutes

Ready time: 30 minutes

Ingredients:
- 4 cups chicken stock
- 2 stalks lemongrass
- 3 kaffir lime leaves
- 2 tablespoons fish sauce
- 2 tablespoons fresh lime juice
- 2 tablespoon brown sugar
- 4 ounces shiitake mushrooms, thinly sliced
- 1 can (8 ounces) straw mushrooms, drained
- 3 tablespoons Thai red curry paste
- 1 cup cooked chicken, cut into small cubes
- 2 tablespoons chopped cilantro
- 2 tablespoons chopped green onions

Instructions:
1. In a large pot, bring the chicken stock to a boil over high heat.
2. Add the lemongrass and kaffir lime leaves, and simmer for 10 minutes.
3. Add the fish sauce, lime juice, brown sugar, shiitake mushrooms, straw mushrooms, and curry paste. Simmer for 10 minutes.
4. Add the chicken and simmer for another 10 minutes.
5. Garnish with cilantro and green onions, and serve.

Nutrition information: Calories-212, Fat-4.5g, Cholesterol-36mg, Sodium-1132mg, Carbohydrate-20g, Protein-20g

31. Indian Chana Masala

Indian Chana Masala is a delicious and spicy dish, originating from Northern India. This savory vegan chickpea curry transforms chickpeas into a flavorful and satisfying meal that is sure to impress! Packed with spices and seasonings, this dish is a flavorful treat that can be enjoyed any time of the year.
Serving: 4
Preparation time: 10 minutes
Ready time: 25 minutes

Ingredients:
- 2 tablespoons coconut oil
- 1 large onion, finely chopped
- 2 cloves garlic, minced
- 2 tablespoons finely minced ginger
- 1 teaspoon ground cumin
- 1 teaspoon ground coriander
- 1/2 teaspoon ground turmeric
- 1/4 teaspoon ground cardamom
- 1/4 teaspoon cayenne pepper
- 2 (15-ounce) cans chickpeas, drained and rinsed
- 1 (14.5-ounce) can diced tomatoes
- 1 cup vegetable broth
- 2 tablespoons tomato paste
- 1/2 cup coconut milk
- 1/2 teaspoon sea salt, or to taste
- Fresh cilantro, for garnish

Instructions:
1. Heat the coconut oil in a large skillet over medium heat. Add the onion and sauté until softened, about 5 minutes.
2. Add the garlic, ginger, cumin, coriander, turmeric, cardamom, and cayenne pepper. Cook for another minute, stirring constantly.
3. Add the chickpeas, diced tomatoes, vegetable broth, tomato paste, and coconut milk to the pan and bring to a simmer.
4. Cover the pan and simmer for 15 to 20 minutes, until the sauce has thickened and the flavors have melded.
5. Remove the pan from the heat and season with sea salt to taste.
6. Garnish with fresh cilantro and serve over steamed basmati rice or quinoa.

Nutrition information: 153 calories, 7g fat, 19g carbohydrates, 4.5g dietary fiber, 7.5g protein.

32. Malaysian Nasi Lemak

Malaysian Nasi Lemak is an iconic dish of Malaysia and is widely served for breakfast and throughout the day. The dish is composed of fragrant

coconut rice accompanied by a selection of side dishes such as fried anchovies, roasted peanuts, hard-boiled eggs, and spicy sambal sauce.
Serving: 6
Preparation Time: 10 minutes
Ready Time: 30 minutes

Ingredients:
- 2 cups jasmine rice
- 2 cups coconut milk
- 3 tablespoons red onion, thinly sliced
- 2 tablespoons vegetable oil
- Fried anchovies
- ½ cup roasted peanuts
- 2 hard-boiled eggs
- Sambal sauce

Instructions:
1. Rinse the jasmine rice and place in a saucepan. Cover the rice with coconut milk and sprinkle with the red onion.
2. Place the pan over medium-high heat and bring to a boil. Once boiling, reduce the heat to low and simmer for 20 minutes.
3. Once the rice is cooked, fluff with a fork and set aside.
4. Heat the vegetable oil in a skillet over medium heat. Fry the anchovies until crispy and set aside.
5. Slice the hard-boiled eggs and set aside.
6. To assemble the dish, spoon the rice into individual serving bowls and top with fried anchovies, roasted peanuts, eggs, and sambal sauce. Serve hot.

Nutrition information: Calories: 450, Fat: 19.6g, Carbohydrates: 57.5g, Protein: 11.6g, Sodium: 677mg

33. Vietnamese Caramelized Clay Pot Fish

Vietnamese Caramelized Clay Pot Fish has a unique savory and slightly sweet taste with a hint of fresh Vietnamese herbs. Served over a bed of warm jasmine rice, it is sure to satisfy. Serving: 4 Preparation Time: 15 minutes Ready Time: 25 minutes

Ingredients:
- 4 (6-ounce) white fish fillets
- 2 tablespoons fish sauce
- 2 tablespoons white sugar
- 1/4 teaspoon black pepper
- 2 tablespoons olive oil
- 1 garlic clove, crushed
- 2 teaspoons grated fresh ginger
- 2 tablespoons fresh cilantro, chopped
- 1/2 cup green onions, chopped

Instructions:
1. In a small bowl, combine the fish sauce, sugar, and pepper, stirring to combine.
2. Heat the olive oil in a medium-sized clay pot over medium heat and add the garlic and ginger. Sauté for 1 minute, then add the fish fillets and fish sauce mixture.
3. Cover the pot and simmer for 15 minutes, or until the fish is cooked through.
4. Uncover the pot and stir in the cilantro and green onions. Let the fish simmer for an additional 5 minutes to reduce the sauce.
5. Serve over warm jasmine rice.

Nutrition information: Calories: 217; Total Fat: 8g; Saturated Fat: 1g; Cholesterol: 44mg; Sodium: 622mg; Carbohydrates: 11g; Dietary Fiber: 1g; Sugar: 6g; Protein: 25g

34. Indonesian Sate Ayam (Chicken Satay)

Indonesian Sate Ayam is a popular dish originating in Indonesia which consists of grilled chicken marinated in a spicy and flavorful sauce. It is often served with a peanut sauce as a dipping sauce and is a great accompaniment to any meal.
Serving: This recipe makes 4 servings of Indonesian Sate Ayam.
Preparation time: This recipe takes about 10 minutes to prepare.
Ready time: The Indonesian Sate Ayam will be ready to eat in about 20 minutes.

Ingredients:
-2 tablespoons of olive oil
-1 pound of boneless, skinless chicken breasts, cut into 1-inch cubes
-2 cloves of garlic, minced
-2 tablespoons of curry powder
-1 teaspoon of turmeric
-1 teaspoon of ground coriander
-2 tablespoons of brown sugar
-2 tablespoons of fish sauce
-1 tablespoon of soy sauce
-1/4 cup of coconut milk
-1/4 cup of peanut butter
-1/4 cup of chopped peanuts, for garnish
-skewers

Instructions:
1. Preheat a grill over medium heat.
2. In a bowl, combine the olive oil, chicken cubes, garlic, curry powder, turmeric, coriander, brown sugar, fish sauce, soy sauce, coconut milk, and peanut butter. Mix until the chicken cubes are evenly coated.
3. Skewer the chicken cubes onto the skewers.
4. Grill the skewered chicken cubes for 10-15 minutes, turning occasionally, until cooked through.
5. Serve the Indonesian Sate Ayam with the chopped peanuts as a garnish.

Nutrition information
Each serving of Indonesian Sate Ayam contains approx. 295 calories, with 15g of fat, 23g of protein, and 7g of carbohydrates.

35. Thai Coconut Curry Noodles (Khao Soi)

This delicious Thai Coconut Curry Noodles (Khao Soi) recipe has all the fragrant and flavorful goodness of traditional Thai curry, but with the added creaminess of a coconut-rich base. A perfect dish for noodle lovers.
Serving: 8

Preparation Time: 10 minutes
Ready Time: 40 minutes

Ingredients:
- 2 tablespoons vegetable oil
- 2 teaspoons brown mustard seeds
- 10 curry leaves
- 2 onions, thinly sliced
- 2 tablespoons Thai red curry paste
- 1 teaspoon ground turmeric
- 1 teaspoon ground coriander
- 1 teaspoon ground cumin
- 2 teaspoons sugar
- 1 teaspoon salt
- 2 cans (13.5 ounces each) full-fat coconut milk
- 2 to 3 cups chicken broth
- 2 tablespoons fish sauce
- 4 boneless, skinless chicken breasts, cut into bite-sized pieces
- 2 packages (17.5 ounces each) (Thai-style) fresh noodles (or 8 ounces dried wide rice noodles)
- 1/2 cup fresh cilantro leaves
- 1/2 cup chopped shallots
- 1/2 cup chopped roasted peanuts

Instructions:
1. Heat the oil in a large Dutch oven or pot over medium heat. Add the mustard seeds and curry leaves and cook for one minute until fragrant.
2. Add the onions and cook for 3 to 5 minutes, stirring, until translucent.
3. Add the curry paste, turmeric, coriander, cumin, sugar and salt and cook for 1 minute.
4. Add the coconut milk and chicken broth and bring the mixture to a simmer. Reduce the heat to low and simmer for 15 minutes.
5. Add the fish sauce and chicken, cover, and simmer for 10 minutes.
6. Meanwhile, cook the noodles according to the package directions.
7. Add the cooked noodles to the curry and stir to combine.
8. Serve the curry with the cilantro, shallots, and peanuts.

Nutrition information:
Calories: 516 kcal, Protein: 28g, Fat: 24g, Carbohydrates: 44g, Fiber: 7g, Sugar: 5g, Sodium: 1622mg

36. Japanese Miso Soup

Japanese miso soup is a savory, slightly sweet, and highly nutritious soup made from a mixture of dashi stock, miso paste, and a variety of Ingredients.
Serving: 4
Preparation time: 10 minutes
Ready time: 25 minutes

Ingredients:
- 4 cups dashi stock
- 4 tablespoons miso paste
- 2 green onions (thinly sliced)
- 2 tablespoons sake
- 4 ounces silken tofu (diced)
- 2 teaspoons ginger (grated)
- 1 teaspoon katsuobushi (bonito flakes)

Instructions:
1. Put the dashi stock in a medium pot over medium heat and bring to a simmer.
2. Reduce the heat to low and add the miso paste, stirring until dissolved.
3. Add the green onions, sake, silken tofu, ginger, and katsuobushi, stirring to combine.
4. Simmer for 5-10 minutes, until all the Ingredients are cooked through and the soup is fragrant.
5. Serve warm.

Nutrition information: Calories: 97, Fat: 4g, Sodium: 775mg, Carbohydrates: 9g, Protein: 5g

37. Korean Japchae

Korean Japchae is a popular Korean dish made from glass noodles (dangmyeon) sautéed with vegetables, meat and a savory sauce. It is a

favorite among Korean banquet dishes and is excellent for potlucks and picnics.
Serving: 4 to 6
Preparation time: 20 minutes
Ready time: 30 minutes

Ingredients:
- 8 ounces dangmyeon noodles
- 2 tablespoons sesame oil
- 2 tablespoons olive oil
- 1/2 teaspoon salt
- 1/2 pound beef, cut into thin strips
- 1/2 pound mushrooms, sliced
- 1 bunch spinach, washed
- 4 cloves garlic, minced
- 1 onion, sliced
- 1 carrot, julienned
- 2 green onions, cut into 2-inch lengths
- 8 tablespoons soy sauce
- 2 tablespoons sugar
- 2 tablespoons sesame seeds

Instructions:
1. In a large pot, bring 8 cups of water to a boil. Add the noodles and cook for 4 to 5 minutes, until the noodles are al dente. Drain and rinse under cold water. Toss the noodles with 1 tablespoon of sesame oil.
2. Heat a large skillet or wok over medium-high heat. Add the olive oil and the salt. Sauté the beef strips in the oil until cooked through, about 6 minutes. Remove from the pan and set aside.
3. In the same skillet, sauté the mushrooms, spinach, garlic, onion and carrot until lightly browned, about 5 minutes. Add the cooked beef, green onions, soy sauce, sugar, and sesame seeds. Stir-fry for 1 to 2 minutes.
4. Add the noodles, stir-fry for an additional 1 to 2 minutes, until the noodles are hot and the sauce is evenly distributed. Taste and adjust seasoning if desired.

Nutrition information
Serving Size: 1/4 of the recipe
Calories: 460

Fat: 14.4 g
Cholesterol: 56.5 mg
Sodium: 1615.9 mg
Carbohydrates: 56.6 g
Fiber: 5.1 g
Protein: 33 g

38. Thai Red Curry with Tofu

Thai Red Curry with Tofu is a vegan dish that is straightforward to make and packed with flavour thanks to the red curry paste. Serve it with some fluffy white rice or jasmine rice and you're in for a delicious dinner.
Serving: 4
Preparation Time: 10 minutes
Ready Time: 30 minutes

Ingredients:
2 tablespoons of vegetable oil
3 tablespoons of Thai red curry paste
2-3 cloves of garlic, minced
1 onion, chopped
1 red bell pepper, chopped
1 can of coconut milk
1 cup of vegetable stock
1 tablespoon of soy sauce
1 teaspoon of brown sugar
1 teaspoon of freshly grated ginger
2 tablespoons of fresh basil leaves
1 block of firm tofu, cubed
1 tablespoon of lime juice

Instructions:
1. Heat the oil in a large pot over medium-high heat.
Add the curry paste and garlic and cook until fragrant.
2. Add the onion and bell pepper and sauté until the vegetables are softened.
3. Pour in the coconut milk and vegetable stock and bring to a simmer.

4. Add the soy sauce, sugar, ginger, basil, and tofu. Simmer for 15 minutes, stirring occasionally.
5. Remove from the heat and add the lime juice.

Nutrition information: (per serving)
Calories: 212 kcal
Fat: 12 g
Carbohydrates: 12.7 g
Protein: 10.3 g
Fiber: 2.7 g

39. Indian Vegetable Curry

Indian Vegetable Curry is a flavorful and fragrant dish, cooked with a blend of herbs and spices. It's a classic one-pot meal that is not just bursting with flavor but is also healthy and perfect for a weeknight dinner.
Serving: 4 servings
Preparation time: 15 minutes
Ready time: 35 minutes

Ingredients:
-2 tablespoons olive oil
-1 onion, diced
-2 cloves garlic, minced
-2 tablespoons grated ginger
-1 teaspoon ground turmeric
-1 teaspoon garam masala
-1 teaspoon chili powder
-1/2 teaspoon ground cumin
-1/4 teaspoon ground cardamom
-2 cups chopped vegetables (carrots, peppers, cauliflower, potatoes, etc.)
-1 can of diced tomatoes
-1 can of light coconut milk
-Salt and pepper to taste

Instructions:
1. Heat the olive oil in a large pan over medium heat.

2. Add the onion and garlic and cook for 5 minutes, stirring often.
3. Stir in the ginger and the spices and cook for an additional minute.
4. Add the chopped vegetables and cook for 5 minutes, stirring occasionally.
5. Add the diced tomatoes, coconut milk, and salt and pepper.
6. Lower the heat and simmer for 20 minutes until the vegetables are tender.
7. Serve with steamed rice and naan.

Nutrition information:
Calories: 200,
Fat: 10 g,
Saturated fat: 4 g,
Carbohydrates: 23 g,
Fiber: 6 g,
Protein: 3 g,
Sodium: 330 mg

40. Malaysian Roti Canai with Curry Sauce

Malaysian roti canai with curry sauce is a wonderfully flavorful dish that is popular in Malaysia. It features a flatbread fried to perfection and served up with a thick and delicious curry sauce. Serve it up with vegetables or other accompaniments for an easy and delicious meal.
Serving: Serves 4
Preparation Time: 45 minutes
Ready Time: 1 hour

Ingredients:
- 2 1/2 cups all-purpose flour
- 1 teaspoon salt
- 2 1/2 tablespoons vegetable oil
- 3/4 cup room temperature water
- 2 tablespoons plain yogurt
- 2 tablespoons butter
- 2 tablespoons vegetable oil, for frying
- 2 medium onions, chopped
- 1 teaspoon garlic, finely chopped

- 1 teaspoon ginger, finely chopped
- 2 teaspoons curry powder
- 1 teaspoon ground coriander
- 1 teaspoon ground cumin
- 1/2 teaspoon chili powder
- 1 can (15 ounces) coconut milk
- 2 tablespoons fish sauce
- 2 tablespoons brown sugar
- 1/2 cup vegetable oil, for deep frying

Instructions:
1. In a large bowl, mix together the flour and salt. Add the vegetable oil, water, and yogurt and mix until the dough comes together. Knead the dough on a lightly floured surface for about 5 minutes. Place the dough in a greased bowl and cover with plastic wrap. Let the dough rest for about 30 minutes.
2. Make the curry sauce by heating the butter and 2 tablespoons vegetable oil in a large skillet over medium heat. Add the onions, garlic, and ginger and cook until the onions are soft, about 5 minutes. Add the curry powder, coriander, cumin, and chili powder and cook for 2 minutes, stirring often.
3. Pour the coconut milk into the skillet and bring to a gentle boil. Cook for 10 minutes, stirring often. Add the fish sauce and brown sugar and cook for 5 more minutes. Turn off the heat and set aside.
4. To make the roti canai, divide the dough into 4 equal pieces. With a floured rolling pin, roll each piece into a thin, 8-inch circle. Heat 1/2 cup vegetable oil in a large skillet over medium heat. Gently place the dough circles in the hot oil and fry until golden brown and crisp, about 2 minutes per side.
5. Remove the roti canais from the skillet and drain on a paper towel-lined plate. Serve warm with the curry sauce and accompaniments of your choice.

Nutrition information: Per Serving - Calories: 324; Total Fat: 24g; Saturated Fat: 10g; Cholesterol: 39mg; Sodium: 504mg; Total Carbohydrate: 21g; Dietary Fiber: 5g; Protein: 4g

41. Vietnamese Shrimp Curry

Vietnamese Shrimp Curry is a rich and flavorful dish, with a medley of spices and aromatics like chilli, cilantro and lemongrass. It's a comforting, economical dish that is quick to make and tasty enough to satisfy a variety of palates.

Serving: 4
Preparation time: 15 minutes
Ready time: 25 minutes

Ingredients:
- 2 tablespoons vegetable oil
- 1 large onion, diced
- 3 cloves garlic, minced
- 3 tablespoons curry powder
- 1/2 teaspoon ground turmeric
- 1 teaspoon salt
- 1 teaspoon black pepper
- 2 tablespoons fish sauce
- 1 (14-ounce) coconut milk
- 8 ounces shrimp, peeled and deveined
- 1 bunch cilantro leaves, for garnish

Instructions:
1. Heat the oil in a large skillet over medium-high heat. Add the onion, garlic, curry powder, turmeric, salt, and black pepper. Cook, stirring constantly, for about 2 minutes or until the vegetables are softened.
2. Pour in the fish sauce and coconut milk and bring the mixture to a simmer.
3. Add the shrimp and cook for about 5 minutes or until the shrimp are cooked through.
4. Taste and adjust the seasoning as desired.
5. Serve garnished with cilantro leaves.

Nutrition information: Per Serving: Calories - 238, Fat - 9g, Saturated Fat - 6g, Cholesterol - 172mg, Sodium - 447mg, Carbohydrates - 9g, Fiber - 2g, Sugar - 2g, Protein - 24g.

42. Indonesian Soto Ayam

Indonesian Soto Ayam is an Indonesian soup made with fresh Ingredients and aromatic spices. It is a comforting, flavorful dish that can be served as lunch or dinner.
Serving: 4
Preparation Time: 30 minutes
Ready Time: 1 hr 10 minutes

Ingredients:
- 2 tablespoons vegetable oil
- 1 onion, diced
- 2 cloves garlic, minced
- 1 teaspoon galangal, minced
- 2 teaspoons ground turmeric
- 2 teaspoons ground coriander
- 2 tablespoons tamarind paste
- 2 teaspoons sugar
- 2 tablespoons fish sauce
- 2 potatoes, quartered
- 2 carrots, peeled and quartered
- 2 cups chicken stock
- 2 cups coconut milk
- 2 boneless, skinless chicken breasts, sliced
- 2 teaspoons sea salt
- 2 teaspoons freshly ground black pepper
- 2 tablespoons chopped fresh cilantro, for garnish

Instructions:
1. Heat the oil in a large pot over medium-high heat.
2. Add the onion and garlic and cook until softened, about 3 minutes.
3. Add the galangal, turmeric, and coriander and cook for 1 minute.
4. Add the tamarind paste, sugar, fish sauce, potatoes, carrots, chicken stock, and coconut milk and bring to a simmer.
5. Add the chicken slices and cook until the chicken is just cooked through, about 15 minutes.
6. Season with salt and pepper and stir in the fresh cilantro.
7. Serve immediately.

Nutrition information: Serving size - 4 people, Calories – 224, Total Fat – 11g (Saturated Fat – 5.1g), Cholesterol – 33 mg, Sodium – 1173mg, Carbohydrates – 19.2 g, Protein – 13.9 g

43. Thai Green Curry with Fish

Thai Green Curry with Fish is a quick and flavorful dish, with fish cooked in a fragrant and spicy coconut-curry sauce. It makes for a flavorful and satisfying meal.
Serving: Serves 4
Preparation time: 10 minutes
Ready time: 30 minutes

Ingredients:
- 1 lb fish fillet (tilapia or white fish)
- 1 can (14 ounces) coconut milk
- 2 - 3 tablespoons green curry paste
- 1 tablespoon vegetable or canola oil
- 2 cloves garlic, minced
- 1 onion, diced
- 1 red bell pepper, diced
- 1 teaspoon sugar
- 1/2 teaspoon salt
- 1/2 teaspoon ground black pepper
- 1/2 cup water
- 2 tablespoons fish sauce
- Juice of 1/2 lime
- Fresh basil, cilantro, or peppers for garnish

Instructions:
1. Heat the oil in a large skillet over medium-high heat.
2. Add the garlic and onion, and cook until softened, about 5 minutes.
3. Add the red bell pepper and cook for an additional 2 minutes.
4. Add the curry paste and stir to coat vegetables.
5. Reduce the heat to medium-low and add the coconut milk and 1/2 cup of water. Simmer for 10 minutes.
6. Season with sugar, salt, and black pepper and add the fish. Simmer for 10-15 minutes, or until the fish is cooked through.

7. Add the fish sauce and lime juice and stir to combine.
8. Taste and adjust seasoning to your preference.
9. Serve in bowls or over rice, and garnish with fresh basil, cilantro, or peppers, if desired.

Nutrition information: Calories: 400, Fat: 25 g, Carbohydrate: 14 g, Protein: 29 g

44. Japanese Curry Udon

Japanese Curry Udon is a tasty and comforting noodle bowl dish that perfectly combines curry and udon in one. It is a popular and common onigiri shop rice ball meal in Japan.
Serving: 4 servings
Preparation time: 15 minutes
Ready time: 30 minutes

Ingredients:
- 1 lb udon noodles
- 2 tablespoons oil
- 1 onion, chopped
- 2 carrots, chopped
- 2 cups beef or chicken broth
- 2 tablespoons curry powder
- 2 tablespoons cornstarch
- 1 teaspoon sugar
- 2 tablespoons soy sauce
- 2 tablespoons mirin
- 2 cups cooked chicken or beef

Instructions:
1. Boil the udon noodles in a pot of water according to the instructions on the package.
2. Heat the oil in a large skillet over medium-high heat. Add the chopped onion and carrots and sauté for about 5 minutes, or until the vegetables are softened.

3. In a medium bowl, whisk together the broth, curry powder, cornstarch, sugar, soy sauce, and mirin. Pour the curry broth mixture into the skillet and simmer for about 10 minutes.
4. Once the curry is done, add in the cooked chicken or beef and simmer for another 5 minutes.
5. Drain the udon noodles and divide into four bowls. Top with the curry and serve.

Nutrition information:
Calories: 367 kcal, Carbohydrates: 55 g, Protein: 19 g, Fat: 8 g, Saturated Fat: 2 g, Cholesterol: 28 mg, Sodium: 950 mg, Potassium: 525 mg, Fiber: 5 g, Sugar: 8 g, Vitamin A: 2381 IU, Vitamin C: 7 mg, Calcium: 63 mg, Iron: 2 mg

45. Korean Dak Galbi (Spicy Stir-fried Chicken)

Korean Dak Galbi is a spicy stir-fried chicken dish that is a popular street food in South Korea. It is flavorful and savory, and very popular among locals and visitors alike.
Serving: 4
Preparation Time: 20 minutes
Ready Time: 30 minutes

Ingredients:
- 600g chicken thigh
- 1 onion, sliced
- 2 stalks spring onion, cut
- 4 cloves garlic, minced
- 2 tablespoons ginger, minced
- 2 tablespoons gochujang (Korean chili paste)
- 2 tablespoons soy sauce
- 2 tablespoons sugar
- 2 tablespoons sesame oil
- 4 tablespoons vegetable oil
- 4 tablespoons rice wine

Instructions:
1. Cut the chicken thigh and onion into cubes.

2. In a large bowl, mix together the marinade of garlic, ginger, gochujang, soy sauce, sugar, sesame oil and rice wine.
3. Place the chicken and onion cubes into the marinade and mix together.
4. Refrigerate the mix for 15 minutes.
5. Heat a large skillet over medium-high heat.
6. Add the vegetable oil and swirl it around the skillet.
7. Add the chicken and onion mix and stir-fry for 5-7 minutes.
8. Add the spring onion and continue to stir-fry for a minute.
9. Serve while hot with steamed rice.

Nutrition information:
Per Serving (about 150g):
- Calories: 244
- Protein: 22g
- Fat: 14g
- carbohydrates: 7g
- cholesterol: 65mg
- sodium: 516mg
- fiber: 1g

46. Singaporean Chili Crab

Singaporean Chili Crab is a popular seafood dish throughout Southeast Asia. It is a savory dish combining the spiciness of chilis, sweetness of tomato sauce, all balanced with the sweetness and brininess of fresh crab. It is a favorite among Singaporeans and a must try for anyone visiting.
Serving: 4-6
Preparation Time: 25 minutes
Ready Time: 1 hour

Ingredients:
- 4 large crabs
- 6 tablespoons vegetable oil
- 3 cloves garlic (minced)
- 2 tablespoons sugar
- 1 teaspoon freshly ground black pepper
- 2 tablespoons chili paste

- 2 tablespoons tomato paste
- 1 cup water
- 3 tablespoons cornstarch
- 2 tablespoons white vinegar
- 2 tablespoons lime juice
- 2 tablespoons fish sauce

Instructions:
1. In a large pot over medium-high heat, add oil and garlic. Cook for about 1 minute, until fragrant.
2. Add the sugar and black pepper, and stir.
3. Add the crab and chili paste, tomato paste, and water. Stir to combine, and bring to a boil.
4. Reduce the heat to low, cover the pot, and simmer for about 20 minutes, until the crabs are tender and cooked through.
5. In a small bowl, whisk together the cornstarch and 2 tablespoons of water until smooth.
6. Gradually add the cornstarch mixture to the pot, stirring constantly.
7. Add the vinegar, lime juice, and fish sauce, and stir to combine.
8. Simmer for an additional 5 minutes, until the sauce thickens.
9. Serve with steamed rice.

Nutrition information: Calories: 276; Protein: 16 g; Fat: 9.3 g; Carbohydrate: 14.6 g; Sodium: 180 mg; Sugar: 10 g

47. Thai Pad Thai

A popular Thai dish, Pad Thai is an easy-to-make meal that's full of flavour. It has a unique balance of sweet, sour and spicy, combined with a variety of fresh and dried Ingredients.
Serving: 2
Preparation time: 10 minutes
Ready time: 20 minutes

Ingredients:
- 225g dried flat noodles
- 3 tablespoons vegetable oil
- 2 tablespoons fish sauce

- 2 tablespoons palm sugar
- 2 cloves garlic
- 1 tablespoon lime juice
- 1 red chilli
- 170g bean sprouts
- 1/2 cup cooked chicken or other protein
- 2 chopped spring onions
- 2 tablespoons crushed peanuts

Instructions:
1. Cook the noodles in boiling water for 5-10 minutes or until tender.
2. Heat the oil in a wok over medium heat. Add the garlic and chilli and fry gently for 1 minute.
3. Add the fish sauce, palm sugar and lime juice and mix together.
4. Add the noodles, chicken, bean sprouts and spring onions and fry for 4-5 minutes, stirring continuously.
5. Serve the Pad Thai on two plates and sprinkle with crushed peanuts.

Nutrition information: Per serving: Energy: 465kcal, Protein: 19.5g, Carbohydrates: 57.2g, Fat: 16.8g, Saturated fat: 2.9g, Fibre: 5.6g, Salt: 2.8g

48. Indian Rogan Josh

Indian Rogan Josh is a aromatic and flavourful South Asian curry originating from Kashmir. A traditional Mughlai dish, this mutton- or lamb-based dish is cooked slowly with yogurt and fragrant Kashmiri spices.
Serving: 4
Preparation Time: 20 minutes
Ready Time: 40 minutes

Ingredients:
- 2 tablespoons vegetable oil
- 2.4 kilograms (5.3 lb) mutton leg, cubed
- 2 tablespoons garlic paste
- 2 tablespoons fresh ginger paste
- 1 (400 grams) tin tomato paste

- 2 tablespoons kashmiri chilli powder
- 2 teaspoons ground cumin
- 1 teaspoon ground coriander
- 1 teaspoon cardamom powder
- 1 teaspoon garam masala
- 2 tablespoons plain yogurt
- 2 cups water
- 2 tablespoons fresh mint leaves, chopped
- Salt, to taste

Instructions:
1. Heat the oil in a large saucepan over high heat.
2. Add the mutton, garlic paste, and ginger paste and cook for 10 minutes, stirring occasionally, until the mutton is lightly browned.
3. Add the tomato paste, chilli powder, cumin, coriander, cardamom powder and garam masala. Stir to combine, and cook for 5 minutes, stirring occasionally.
4. Add the yogurt and stir well. Reduce the heat to low and simmer for 15 minutes, stirring occasionally.
5. Add the water and simmer for 15 minutes. Add the mint leaves and season to taste with salt.
6. Serve hot with steamed basmati rice or naan bread.

Nutrition information:
Calories: 366, Fat: 20.5g, Sodium: 113mg, Total Carbohydrates: 10g, Protein: 33g.

49. Malaysian Mee Goreng

Malaysian Mee Goreng is a delicious Malaysian stir-fried noodle dish that is full of flavor and spice. It is a popular Southeast-Asian dish enjoyed by many people around the world.
Serving: 4
Preparation Time: 10 minutes
Ready Time: 15 minutes

Ingredients:
- 2 tablespoons vegetable oil

- 500 grams diced beef
- 10 shallots, finely chopped
- 2 cloves garlic, minced
- 1 teaspoon shrimp paste
- 4 dried chilies
- 2 tablespoons light soy sauce
- 2 tablespoons dark soy sauce
- 2 tablespoons sweet soy sauce
- 500 grams yellow noodles
- 1 tomato, julienned
- 1/2 red bell pepper, julienned
- 1 cup bean sprouts
- 2 tablespoons lime juice

Instructions:
1. Heat the oil in a large wok over medium high heat.
2. Add the beef and cook, stirring frequently, until lightly browned.
3. Add the shallots, garlic, and shrimp paste to the wok and stir-fry for 1 minute.
4. Add the chilies, soy sauces, and noodles to the wok and stir-fry for an additional 2 minutes.
5. Add the tomato, bell pepper, bean sprouts, and lime juice to the wok and stir-fry for a final 2 minutes.
6. Serve the Malaysian Mee Goreng immediately.

Nutrition information: (Per Serving)
- Calories: 545
- Fat: 20g
- Saturated Fat: 4g
- Cholesterol: 68mg
- Sodium: 1306mg
- Carbohydrates: 62g
- Fiber: 3g
- Sugar: 7g
- Protein: 33g

50. Vietnamese Lemongrass Beef Curry

Vietnamese Lemongrass Beef Curry is a delicious and flavorful dish, traditional to Vietnamese cuisine. This savory curry is made with rich, aromatic flavors such as coconut milk, lemongrass, and ginger.

Serving: Serves 4
Preparation Time: 15 minutes
Ready Time: 35 minutes

Ingredients:
- 1/2 lb. beef (sirloin or tenderloin, sliced thinly)
- 2 tablespoons vegetable oil
- 2 shallots (minced)
- 2 cloves garlic (minced)
- 3 tablespoons red curry paste
- 1 1/2 tablespoons lemongrass (minced)
- 1 teaspoon ginger (minced)
- 2 cups coconut milk
- 2 tablespoons fish sauce
- 2 teaspoons brown sugar
- 1 teaspoon red pepper flakes
- 1/4 cup tamari
- 2 tablespoons fresh cilantro (minced)
- 2 tablespoons fresh mint (minced)

Instructions:
1. Heat the oil in a medium saucepan over medium heat.
2. Add the beef and cook until lightly browned, about 5 minutes.
3. Add the shallots, garlic, curry paste, lemongrass, and ginger. Cook until fragrant, about 3 minutes.
4. Add the coconut milk, fish sauce, brown sugar, and red pepper flakes. Stir to combine.
5. Bring the mixture to a simmer and cook 15 minutes, stirring occasionally.
6. Once the curry has thickened, add the tamari and season to taste with salt and pepper.
7. Remove the curry from the heat and stir in the cilantro and mint.
8. Serve over white long grain rice.

Nutrition information:
- Calories: 514
- Fat: 30 g

- Sodium: 1222 mg
- Carbohydrates: 22 g
- Protein: 37 g

51. Indonesian Beef Rendang with Coconut Rice

Indonesian Beef Rendang with Coconut Rice is an Indonesian dish made with a spicy beef curry and coconut rice.
Serving: Serves 4
Preparation Time: 30 minutes
Ready Time: 1 hour

Ingredients:
2 lbs stewing beef, cubed
1 onion, chopped
3 cloves garlic, diced
1" piece of ginger, grated
2 Tbsp Coconut oil
1 tsp ground turmeric
1 tsp ground fennel
1 tsp ground cinnamon
1 tsp cardamom
1 tsp ground star anise
1/2 tsp cayenne pepper
1/2 tsp ground cloves
1-14 oz can Coconut Milk
1/2 cup water
2 cups uncooked long grain rice

Instructions:
1. In a large pan, heat the coconut oil.
2. Add the onion, garlic, and ginger to the pan and sauté for a few minutes until the onion is soft.
3.
Add the beef and the spices and sauté the mixture for 5 minutes.
4. Add the coconut milk and water and bring to a boil.
5. Reduce the heat to low and cover the pan with a lid and simmer for an hour.

6. In a separate pan, cook 2 cups of rice according to the package instructions.
7. Serve the beef rendang with the coconut rice.

Nutrition information: per serving: 294 calories, 11.5 g fat, 26.2 g protein, 24.6 g carbs, 1.4 g fiber

52. Thai Pumpkin Curry

Thai Pumpkin Curry is a yellow-colored curry cooked with a variety of Thai herbs and spices creating a unique and delicious flavor.
Serving: 6
Preparation Time: 10 minutes
Ready Time: 25 minutes

Ingredients:
- 1 pound pumpkin (cubed)
- 2 tablespoons vegetable oil
- 1/2 teaspoon ground turmeric
- 1/2 teaspoon ground coriander
- 2 tablespoons red curry paste
- 1 can (14 ounces) coconut milk
- 2 tablespoons fish sauce
- 2 tablespoons brown sugar
- 4 green onions (sliced)
- 1/2 cup fresh basil (chopped)

Instructions:
1. Heat oil in a large skillet over medium heat. Add in pumpkin cubes, turmeric, and ground coriander and stir until coated in oil. Cook for 5 minutes.
2. Add red curry paste, coconut milk, fish sauce, and brown sugar. Bring to a simmer and cook for 15 minutes.
3. Add green onions and basil, stir until combined. Simmer for an additional 5 minutes.
4. Serve over rice or noodles.

Nutrition information:

Serving Size 6,
Calories 240, Fat 18g (Saturated 16g), Cholesterol 0mg, Sodium 880mg, Carbohydrates 20g (Fiber 4g, Sugars 9g), Protein 4g

53. Japanese Beef Curry

Japanese beef curry is an easy and delicious hearty meal that blends beef with fragrant curry and vegetables. Serve it over a bed of steamed rice for a satisfying meal.
Serving: Serves 4
Preparation Time: 15 minutes
Ready Time: 40 minutes

Ingredients:
-1 tablespoon vegetable oil
-2 medium onions, diced
-1 pound lean ground beef
-2 cloves garlic, minced
-3 tablespoons curry powder
-1 teaspoon ground ginger
-1 teaspoon sugar
-14.5 ounces (1 can) diced tomatoes
-5 ounces frozen mixed vegetables
-2 1/2 cups beef broth
-1/2 teaspoon salt

Instructions:
1. Heat the oil in a large skillet over medium-high heat.
2. Add the onions and cook until softened, about 5 minutes.
3. Add the ground beef and garlic and cook until the beef is cooked through, about 5 minutes.
4. Add the curry powder, ginger, sugar, tomatoes, mixed vegetables, broth, and salt. Bring to a boil.
5. Reduce the heat to low, cover, and simmer for 30 minutes or until the vegetables are cooked.
6. Serve over cooked rice and garnish with fresh parsley, if desired.

Nutrition information:

Per Serving:
290 calories, 12.2g fat, 26.5g protein, 15.4g carbohydrates, 3.3g fiber, 517mg sodium.

54. Korean Bibimbap

Korean Bibimbap is a classic Korean recipe that combines a mix of vegetables, seasoned beef, and a deliciously sunny-side up egg, all served atop a bed of warm white rice.
 Serving: Serves 4
 Preparation Time: 15 minutes
 Ready Time: 45 minutes

Ingredients:
- 4 cups steamed white rice
- ½ pound ground beef
- 2 tablespoons sesame oil
- 2 tablespoons soy sauce
- 1 carrot, julienned
- ½ cucumber, julienned
- 2 zucchinis, julienned
- 1 bean sprout, julienned
- 4 eggs
- 1 teaspoon gochujang (Korean red pepper sauce)

Instructions:
1. Heat a large skillet over medium-high heat and add the ground beef.
2. Cook the beef for 5 minutes, stirring occasionally, until cooked through and lightly browned.
3. Add the sesame oil, soy sauce, carrot, cucumber, zucchini, and bean sprouts and stir to combine.
4. Cook for an additional 5 minutes until the vegetables are lightly cooked and the beef is lightly browned.
5. In a separate skillet, heat 1 teaspoon of canola oil over medium-high heat.
6. Crack the eggs and cook for 2-3 minutes until the whites are set and the yolks runny.
7. Remove the egg from the heat.

8. Divide the warm rice between 4 bowls and top with the beef and vegetables.
9. Garnish with the cooked egg and gochujang sauce and serve.

Nutrition information:
Serving size: 1 bowl | Calories: 482 kcal | Carbohydrates: 42 g | Protein: 24 g | Fat: 22 g | Saturated Fat: 8 g | Cholesterol: 150 mg | Sodium: 559 mg | Potassium: 659 mg | Fiber: 4 g | Sugar: 5 g | Vitamin A: 2255 IU | Vitamin C: 35.2 mg | Calcium: 97 mg | Iron: 2.6 mg

55. Singaporean Black Pepper Crab

This Singaporean Black Pepper Crab recipe is a classic seafood dish, with whole crab cooked in a spicy and flavorful black pepper sauce. This dish is sure to become a favorite.
Serving: 4
Preparation Time: 15 minutes
Ready Time: 35 minutes

Ingredients:
- 4 1-pound live crabs
- 1/4 cup peanut oil
- 4 tablespoons fresh ginger, minced
- 8 cloves garlic, minced
- 1 tablespoon black peppercorns, crushed
- 2 tablespoons fish sauce
- 2 tablespoons light soy sauce
- 1/4 cup chicken or seafood stock
- 2 tablespoons cornstarch
- 2 tablespoons spring onions, sliced

Instructions:
1. Clean the crabs and remove the gills and innards. Crack the shells and halve them.
2. Heat the oil in a wok or large frying pan over medium-high heat. Add the ginger and garlic and stir-fry for 30 seconds.
3. Add the pepper, fish sauce, soy sauce, and stock. Simmer for 3-5 minutes.

4. Add the crabs and stir-fry for 5 minutes. Transfer the contents of the wok to a high-sided baking dish.
5. Make a slurry with the cornstarch and 2 tablespoons of water. Stir it into the sauce in the wok and simmer for a few minutes until thickened.
6. Pour the sauce over the crabs and top with the spring onions. Bake at 350°F for 15-20 minutes or until the crabs are just cooked through.

Nutrition information: Calories: 400; Fat: 22g; Saturated Fat: 4g; Cholesterol: 109mg; Sodium: 1639mg; Carbohydrates: 18g; Fiber: 2g; Protein: 25g

56. Thai Tom Kha Gai (Coconut Chicken Soup)

Thai Tom Kha Gai, also known as Coconut Chicken Soup, is a classic Thai soup prepared with rich coconut milk, savory lemongrass, lime leaves, and ginger. The traditional dish is filled with flavor and is uniquely comforting and soothing.
Serving: Serves 6
Preparation time: 10 minutes
Ready time: 35 minutes

Ingredients:
- 2 cans (13.5 oz each) coconut milk
- 2 cups chicken broth
- 4 tablespoons fish sauce
- 2 stalks fresh lemongrass, cut into 1-in pieces
- 2 kaffir lime leaves
- 2 fresh Thai chiles, chopped
- 2 tablespoons vegetable oil
- 4 cloves garlic, minced
- 2 tablespoons minced fresh ginger
- 1 lb boneless, skinless chicken thighs, cut into 1-inch pieces
- 1/4 cup fresh lime juice
- 1/4 cup packed fresh cilantro leaves

Instructions:
1. In a medium saucepan, bring the coconut milk, chicken broth, fish sauce, lemongrass, and kaffir lime leaves to a gentle boil over medium

heat, stirring occasionally. Reduce heat to low, partially cover, and simmer for 20 minutes.
2. Heat oil in a large skillet over medium heat. Add garlic and ginger and cook until fragrant, about 30 seconds. Add the chicken pieces and cook, stirring occasionally, until no longer pink, about 5 minutes.
3. Add the chicken to the saucepan with the broth and simmer for an additional 5 minutes.
4. Remove the broth from the heat and stir in the lime juice and cilantro.
5. Serve hot with steamed rice.

Nutrition information
Calories: 288Fat: 21 gTotal Carbohydrate: 5.3 gProtein: 16.4 gSodium: 831 mgFiber: 0.7 g

57. Indian Palak Paneer

This easy, delicious and fragrant Indian Palak Paneer recipe is the perfect vegetarian twist to your everyday paneer curry. Serve it with rice or flatbread and enjoy!
Serving: 4
Preparation time: 15 minutes
Ready time: 25 minutes

Ingredients:
- 200g Paneer (cottage cheese)
- 2 tablespoons coconut oil or butter
- 2 teaspoons Cumin
- 2 teaspoons Coriander powder
- 1 teaspoon Garam Masala
- 1 teaspoon turmeric
- 2 cloves garlic, finely minced
- 1/2 teaspoon Ginger
- 2 teaspoons tomato puree
- 2 Green chilies, sliced
- 1 Onion, diced
- 2 cups Spinach, washed and chopped
- Salt, to taste
- 2 tablespoons Cream

- 2 tablespoons Coriander, chopped

Instructions:
1. Heat the coconut oil or butter in a deep pan. When it is hot, add cumin, coriander powder, garam masala, and turmeric. Stir it for a few seconds.
2. Add garlic, ginger, and green chili. Stir for a minute until the mixture is fragrant.
3. Add the onion and cook it for 3-4 minutes, until it is softened.
4. Add the tomato puree and spinach and cook for 5 minutes until the spinach is tender.
5. Add the paneer cubes and mix everything together. Add salt to taste.
6. Add cream and chopped coriander and simmer for another 5 minutes.

Nutrition information: Per serving: Calories – 296, Fat – 18g, Carbohydrates – 11g, Protein – 22g.

58. Malaysian Curry Puffs

Malaysian Curry Puffs are delicious savory snacks that are easy to make and full of flavor. This traditional East-Asian dish is a favorite among many.
Serving: Makes 12 puffs
Preparation Time: 15 minutes
Ready Time: 45 minutes

Ingredients:
- 1 package frozen puff pastry
- 2 tablespoons vegetable oil
- ½ cup yellow onion, chopped
- ½ teaspoon ground turmeric
- 1 teaspoon garlic powder
- 2 teaspoons grated fresh ginger
- 1 teaspoon ground cumin
- 1 teaspoon ground coriander
- 2 tablespoons curry powder
- 1 cup cooked potatoes, mashed
- ½ cup cooked carrots, chopped

- ½ cup cooked peas, chopped
- Salt and freshly ground black pepper

Instructions:
1. Preheat oven to 400°F.
2. Heat vegetable oil in a large pan over medium heat. Add onion, turmeric, garlic powder, ginger, cumin, and coriander. Cook until vegetables are softened, about 5 minutes. Stir in curry powder and cook for 1 minute.
3. Add potatoes, carrots, and peas to pan. Season with salt and pepper, to taste. Cook for 3 minutes, stirring occasionally, until vegetables are warmed through. Remove from heat and set aside.
4. Cut puff pastry sheets into 12 squares and place onto a baking sheet lined with parchment paper.
5. Spoon curry mixture onto the center of each pastry square. Fold the corners together and press to seal.
6. Bake in preheated oven for 25 minutes or until puffs are golden brown.
7. Serve warm.

Nutrition information:
Calories: 135 kcal, Carbohydrates: 15 g, Protein: 3 g, Fat: 7 g, Cholesterol: 0 mg, Sodium: 80 mg, Potassium: 122 mg, Fiber: 1 g, Sugar: 1 g.

59. Vietnamese Shaking Beef (Bo Luc Lac)

Vietnamese Shaking Beef (Bo Luc Lac) is a popular, flavorful dish that is simple to make and highly nutritious. It is made by marinating thinly sliced beef in a blend of garlic, fish sauce, and lime before grilling, then tossing it with a flavorful Asian garlic-lime sauce.
Serving: 4-6
Preparation time: 25 minutes
Ready time: 30 minutes

Ingredients:
- 1 lb. top sirloin steak, thinly sliced
- 4 cloves garlic, minced

- 1/4 cup lime juice
- 1 tablespoon fish sauce
- 2 tablespoons vegetable oil
- 4 tablespoons fresh cilantro, chopped
- 2 tablespoons butter
- 2 teaspoons brown sugar
-2 tablespoons oyster sauce

Instructions:
1. In a large bowl, combine steak, garlic, lime juice, and fish sauce; marinate for at least 15 minutes.
2. Heat a wok or skillet over medium-high heat; add vegetable oil.
3. Add steak mixture and cook until steak is lightly browned.
4. Add cilantro, butter, and brown sugar; toss well to incorporate.
5. Remove from heat and add oyster sauce; stir to combine.
6. Plate and serve.

Nutrition information:
Calories: 245, Protein: 21.7g, Carbohydrates: 5.5g, Fat: 15.1g, Fiber: 0.7g, Sugar: 3g, Cholesterol: 62mg, Sodium: 353mg

60. Indonesian Nasi Uduk

Indonesian Nasi Uduk is a beloved traditional rice dish served in the Indonesian archipelago. It is made with coconut milk and a variety of spices, giving it a unique and delicious flavor.
Serving: 4
Preparation Time: 15 minutes
Ready Time: 40 minutes

Ingredients:
- 2 cups of Jasmine rice
- 2 cups of coconut milk
- 2 cups of water
- 2 tablespoons of vegetable oil
- 1/4 teaspoon of turmeric
- 1/2 teaspoon of salt
- 1 small bay leaf

- 1 lime, sliced
- 1/4 teaspoon of ground cloves
- 1/4 teaspoon of ground cinnamon

Instructions:
1. Rinse the Jasmine rice in a colander until the water runs clear.
2. Heat the vegetable oil in a pot over medium heat.
3. Add the rice, turmeric, salt, bay leaf, cloves and cinnamon and mix everything together.
4. Pour in the coconut milk and the water and stir until combined.
5. Reduce the heat and cover with a lid. Let the rice simmer for 35 minutes.
6. Once the liquid is absorbed, remove from the heat and allow to cool.
7. Garnish with lime slices.

Nutrition information:
Calories: 330, Total Fat: 18g, Cholesterol: 0mg, Sodium: 480mg, Total Carbohydrates: 36g, Dietary Fiber: 2g, Sugar 3g, Protein: 5g.

61. Thai Massaman Curry with Chicken

For a warm and flavorful dinner, Thai Massaman Curry with Chicken is a great choice. It is a combination of tender chicken, potatoes, and peanuts in a spicy, yet sweet, Massaman-style curry sauce, and it is served with steamed rice. Serving: 4 to 6 Preparation Time: 15 minutes Ready Time: 45 minutes

Ingredients:
- 2 ½ tablespoons Thai Massaman Curry Paste
- 2 tablespoons coconut oil
- 1 package (12 ounces) boneless, skinless chicken thighs, cut into 1-inch pieces
- 2 cloves garlic, minced
- 2 tablespoons fish sauce
- 1 ½ tablespoons brown sugar
- ¼ teaspoon ground cloves
- 1 can (14 ounces) light unsweetened coconut milk
- 1 can (14 ounces) bamboo shoots, drained

- 2 cups small potatoes, cubed
- 1 small red bell pepper, cut into cubes
- ¾ cup roasted peanuts

Instructions:

1. In a small bowl, mix together the Massaman curry paste, coconut oil, garlic, fish sauce, brown sugar, and ground cloves.
2. Heat a large skillet or wok over medium heat. Add the chicken and cook for 4-5 minutes, until golden brown.
3. Add the curry paste mixture to the skillet. Cook, stirring, for 2 minutes.
4. Add the coconut milk, bamboo shoots, potatoes, and bell pepper. Bring to a boil, then reduce the heat and simmer, stirring occasionally, for 20-25 minutes, or until the potatoes and chicken are cooked through.
5. Serve over steamed white or brown rice, and top with the roasted peanuts.

Nutrition information:
Calories: 250
Total fat: 9.4g
Saturated fat: 6.0g
Cholesterol: 50mg
Sodium: 430mg
Carbohydrates: 24g
Fiber: 2.4g
Sugar: 5.2g
Protein: 16.9g

62. Japanese Okonomiyaki

Japanese Okonomiyaki is a savory Japanese-style pancake that is filled with vegetables and other ingredients then topped with flavorful sauces.
Serving: 4-6
Preparation time: 10 minutes
Ready time: 30 minutes

Ingredients:
- 4 cups cabbage, finely shredded

- 2 cups all-purpose flour
- 2 eggs
- 4 tablespoons fish sauce or soy sauce
- 1 teaspoon sesame oil
- 2 tablespoons vegetable oil
- Toppings of choice (mayonnaise, katsuobushi - dried bonito flakes, aonori – dried seaweed, beni shoga– pickled ginger, etc.)

Instructions:
1. In a large bowl, mix together the cabbage, flour, eggs, fish or soy sauce, and sesame oil.
2. Heat the vegetable oil in a large non-stick skillet over medium-high heat.
3. Place a heaping scoop of the Okonomiyaki batter into the hot skillet and spread it into a thin pancake with a spatula.
4. Reduce heat to medium-low, cover the skillet with a lid, and let it cook for about 8 minutes, or until the pancake is lightly golden in color.
5. Flip the pancake over with a spatula and cook it for an additional 8 minutes.
6. Remove the pancake from the heat and transfer it to a large plate.
7. Add the desired toppings, such as mayonnaise, katsuobushi, aonori, beni shoga, etc.

Nutrition information: Per Serving: Calories – 379.3, Total Fat – 12.8g, Cholesterol – 67.3mg, Sodium – 808.2mg, Carbohydrates – 52.1g, Protein – 13.6g.

63. Korean Army Stew (Budae Jjigae)

Korean Army Stew (Budae Jjigae), also known as "army base stew," is a popular Korean dish made with a variety of stir-fried ingredients such as ham, sausage, spam, kimchi, and ramen noodles. This flavorful stew is comforting, filling, and sure to please any crowd.
Serving: Serves 4
Preparation time: 10 minutes
Ready time: 25 minutes

Ingredients:

- 2 tablespoons vegetable oil
- 1 pound ham, diced
- 12 ounces spam, diced
- 4 ounces sausage, diced
- 4 cups water
- 1 package ramen noodles, broken into smaller pieces
- 2-3 cups kimchi, chopped
- 1/4 cup gochujang (Korean chili paste)
- 2 green onions, diced
- 2 tablespoons sesame oil

Instructions:
1. Heat the vegetable oil in a large pot over medium heat.
2. Add the ham, spam, and sausage and cook, stirring occasionally, until the meat is lightly browned, about 10 minutes.
3. Add the water and bring to a boil.
4. Add the ramen noodles and kimchi and reduce the heat to low. Simmer for 15 minutes.
5. Stir in the gochujang, green onions, and sesame oil and simmer for an additional 5 minutes.
6. Serve warm with rice or kimchi pancake.

Nutrition information:
Calories: 403 kcal, Carbohydrates: 15 g, Protein: 32 g, Fat: 24 g, Saturated Fat: 5 g, Trans Fat: 1 g, Cholesterol: 76 mg, Sodium: 1406 mg, Potassium: 262 mg, Fiber: 0 g, Sugar: 3 g, Vitamin A: 163 IU, Vitamin C: 4 mg, Calcium: 32 mg, Iron: 2 mg

64. Singaporean Fish Head Curry

Singaporean Fish Head Curry is a delicious blend of spices, vegetables, and herbs, creating a unique curry dish that combines sweet and spicy elements. The fish head lends a delicious flavor that is sure to be a hit with any fish lover.
Serving: 4-6
Preparation Time: 15 minutes
Ready Time: 1 hour

Ingredients:
- 1 (2-pound) whole fish head
- 1 onion, diced
- 2 cloves of garlic, minced
- 2 tablespoons vegetable oil
- 1 teaspoon ground turmeric
- 1 teaspoon ground cumin
- 1 teaspoon ground coriander
- 1 teaspoon chili powder
- 1 teaspoon salt
- 1/2 teaspoon black pepper
- 2 large tomatoes, diced
- 1 small red bell pepper, diced
- 2 tablespoons chopped fresh cilantro
- 4 cups water

Instructions:
1. Heat the oil in a large pot over medium heat.
2. Add the onion, garlic, turmeric, cumin, coriander, chili powder, salt, and black pepper. Cook for about 5 minutes, stirring often.
3. Add the tomato and bell pepper and cook for about 3 minutes.
4. Add the fish head and cook for about 5 minutes.
5. Add the water and bring the mixture to a boil. Reduce the heat to a simmer and cook for about 30 minutes.
6. Add the cilantro and stir to combine.
7. Serve over rice or with naan.

Nutrition information: Per serving: 330 calories; 16.5 g fat; 10.2 g carbohydrates; 25.9 g protein; 6.4 g fiber

65. Thai Red Curry with Vegetables

This Thai red curry with vegetables is one of the most soul-satisfying dishes that you can make at home. It is incredibly flavorful and is sure to be enjoyed by the whole family.
Serving: 4
Preparation Time: 10-15 minutes
Ready Time: 30-35 minutes

Ingredients:
- 1 tablespoon canola oil
- ½ red onion, diced
- 2 bell peppers, diced
- 4 cloves garlic, minced
- 2 tablespoons fresh ginger, minced
- 2 tablespoons Thai red curry paste
- 4 tablespoons soy sauce
- 200g cauliflower, cut into florets
- 4-5 kaffir lime leaves
- 1 can (400ml) coconut milk
- 2 tablespoons lime juice
- 2 tablespoons brown sugar
- Salt and pepper to taste

Instructions:
1. Heat oil in a large skillet over medium high heat.
2. Add onion, bell peppers and garlic, sautéing until vegetables are tender, about 5-7 minutes.
3. Add ginger, curry paste, and soy sauce. Sauté for another minute or two until the paste is fragrant.
4. Add cauliflower and kaffir lime leaves, stirring to combine.
5. Pour in the coconut milk and bring it to a gentle simmer.
6. Reduce the heat and simmer, stirring occasionally, for 10-15 minutes.
7. Add lime juice, brown sugar, and season with salt and pepper to taste.
8. Simmer for another 5 minutes, or until the vegetables are cooked through and the sauce has thickened.

Nutrition information: Each serving of Thai Red Curry with vegetables is approximately 300 calories and contains:
- 16.7g of Protein
- 19.3g of fat
- 19.1g of Carbohydrates
- 6.2g of Sugar
- 4.7g of Fibre
- 431mg of Sodium

66. Indian Tandoori Chicken

Indian tandoori chicken is a classic Indian dish that consists of marinated chicken cooked in a clay oven called a tandoor. It is served with either a lemon-yogurt sauce or a creamy tomato sauce. Serving: 4 Preparation time: 20 min Ready time: 1-2 hrs

Ingredients:
2 lb. boneless, skinless chicken breasts, cut into large pieces
- 1 cup plain yogurt or Greek yogurt
- 2 tbsp. freshly squeezed lemon juice
- 2 cloves garlic, minced
- 1" piece ginger, minced
- 2 tsp. garam masala
- 1 tsp. cumin
- 1 tsp. paprika
- 1 tsp. red chilli powder
- 1/2 tsp. turmeric
- 1/4 cup vegetable oil
- Salt and pepper

Instructions:
1. In a bowl, add the yogurt, lemon juice, garlic, ginger, garam masala, cumin, paprika, red chili powder, turmeric, vegetable oil, salt and pepper.
2. Mix all the Ingredients together until a homogeneous paste forms.
3. Place the chicken pieces in a large bowl and pour the prepared paste over them.
4. Use your hands to massage the paste into the chicken pieces, making sure all of them are coated completely
5. Cover and place in the refrigerator to marinate for 1-2 hours.
6. Preheat your oven to 350°F and brush a baking sheet with some oil.
7. Place the chicken pieces on the baking sheet, making sure none of them is touching each other.
8. Bake for 25-30 minutes or until the chicken is cooked through.
9. Serve with a side of lemon-yogurt sauce or a creamy tomato sauce.

Nutrition information:
Calories: 279, Fat:10g, Saturated Fat: 1.5g, Carbohydrates: 5g, Protein: 34g, Sugar: 1.5g, Fiber: 0g, Cholesterol: 87mg, Sodium: 288mg

67. Malaysian Prawn Noodles (Hokkien Mee)

Malaysian prawn noodles (Hokkien Mee) is a traditional Chinese-Malaysian noodle dish, famous for its savory and spicy flavors. This delicious and flavorful dish is a wonderful way to enjoy the flavors of Southeast Asia!

Serving: 4
Preparation Time: 30 minutes
Ready Time: 45 minutes

Ingredients:
- 400g fresh egg noodles
- 2 cloves minced garlic
- 4 tablespoons vegetable oil
- 400g medium-sized peeled prawns
- 2 tablespoons dark soy sauce
- 2 tablespoons oyster sauce
- 1 teaspoon sugar
- 1 teaspoon sesame oil
- 2 cups chicken broth
- 2 cups sliced mushrooms
- 1 cup diced onions
- 2 tablespoons chopped cilantro
- 3 tablespoons fish sauce

Instructions:
1. Heat the oil in a wok over medium heat.
2. Add the garlic and sauté for a few seconds.
3. Add the prawns and stir fry for about 2 minutes, or until the prawns turn pink and are cooked through.
4. Add the soy sauce, oyster sauce, sugar, sesame oil and chicken broth. Simmer for 5 minutes.
5. Add the mushrooms, onions and cilantro and simmer for an additional 5 minutes.
6. Add the noodles and fish sauce and cook for 3 minutes, stirring often.
7. Garnish with additional cilantro and serve.

Nutrition information: Per serving, Malaysian Prawn Noodles (Hokkien Mee) provides approximately 318 Calories, 17g Fat, 35g Carbohydrates, and 18g Protein.

68. Vietnamese Chicken Curry

Vietnamese Chicken Curry is a classic, delicious and aromatic dish that combines the flavors of lemongrass, garlic, sweet potatoes and coconut milk. It's easy to make and sure to please.
Serving: 4-5
Preparation Time: 20 minutes
Ready Time: 40 minutes

Ingredients:
1 tbsp vegetable oil
2 cloves garlic, minced
1 small onion, diced
2 lemongrass stalks, minced
1 lb chicken thighs, cut into bite-size pieces
1 medium sweet potato, peeled and diced
1 cup coconut milk
3 tbsp fish sauce
2 tsp curry powder
1 tsp white sugar
1/4 tsp ground black pepper

Instructions:
1. In a large skillet or saucepan over medium-high heat, add the oil and garlic. Fry until the garlic begins to become fragrant.
2. Add the onion and lemongrass and cook until softened, about 5 minutes.
3. Add the chicken and sweet potato and cook until the chicken is opaque, about 5 minutes.
4. Add the coconut milk, fish sauce, curry powder, sugar, and pepper, and bring to a boil.
5. Reduce the heat to low and simmer, stirring occasionally, for 25-30 minutes, or until the chicken and potatoes are cooked through.

Nutrition information: per serving, 250 calories, 12g fat, 9g carbohydrates, 24g protein.

69. Indonesian Beef Satay

Indonesian Beef Satay is a delicious skewered beef dish that is popular in Southeast Asian cuisine. It is marinated in an aromatic blend of soy sauce, garlic, and ginger before being cooked over a charcoal fire for a smoky flavor. Served alongside a flavorful peanut sauce, this tasty dish is sure to please everyone at the dinner table!
Serving: 4
Preparation time: 3 hours
Ready time: 30 minutes

Ingredients:
- 2 lbs of lean ground beef
- 1/4 cup of light soy sauce
- 3 cloves of minced garlic
- 1 tablespoon of grated fresh ginger
- 8 to 10 wooden skewers
- Peanut sauce for Serving:

Instructions:
1. In a large bowl, combine the beef, soy sauce, garlic and ginger and mix together to evenly combine the Ingredients.
2. Soak the wooden skewers in a bowl of water for 30 minutes.
3. Thread the beef onto the wooden skewers and place onto a plate.
4. Preheat the grill to medium-high.
5. Place the beef skewers onto the preheated grill and cook for 8 to 10 minutes, or until cooked through.
6. Turn the skewers occasionally to prevent burning.
7. Serve the cooked satay skewers with peanut sauce on the side.

Nutrition information: Per serving, Indonesian Beef Satay contains approximately 365 calories, 22g of protein, 11g of carbohydrates, and 24g of fat.

70. Thai Pineapple Fried Rice

Thai Pineapple Fried Rice is a classic dish staple in Southeast Asian cuisine. The dish is fragrant and flavorful, with its subtle sweetness deriving from the combination of flavors and the use of fresh pineapple.
Serving: 4
Preparation time: 15 minutes
Ready time: 35 minutes

Ingredients:
- 2 tablespoons vegetable oil
- 2 eggs, beaten
- 1/4 cup onion, diced
- 1/2 cup cashews
- 1/4 cup carrots, diced
- 2 cloves garlic, minced
- 1/4 cup green peas
- 2 cups cooked jasmine rice
- 2 tablespoons soy sauce
- 2 tablespoons fish sauce
- 2 tablespoons lime juice
- 1/2 cup pineapple, diced
- 1 teaspoon sugar
- Salt and pepper, to taste

Instructions:
1. Heat the oil in a wok over medium-high heat.
2. Once the oil is hot, add in the eggs and scramble them.
3. Add in the onion and cashews and fry for 1 minute.
4. Add in the carrots and garlic and fry for 1 minute.
5. Then stir in the peas and cooked rice and fry for 2 minutes.
6. Next, add in the soy sauce, fish sauce, lime juice, pineapple, sugar, salt, and pepper and fry for another 3 minutes.
7. Serve hot.

Nutrition information: Calories: 384 kcal, Total Fat: 14 g, Saturated Fat: 4 g, Cholesterol: 81 mg, Sodium: 734 mg, Potassium: 176 mg, Carbohydrates: 51 g, Fiber: 3 g, Sugar: 10 g, Protein: 9 g

71. Japanese Miso Eggplant (Nasu Dengaku)

Japanese Miso Eggplant (Nasu Dengaku) is an incredibly tasty and easy to make dish. It's got a wonderful balance of sweet and savory flavors that are sure to please the palate. It's the perfect dish to prepare for a weeknight dinner.
Serving: 2
Preparation Time: 10 minutes
Ready Time: 40 minutes

Ingredients:
- 2 eggplants
- 2 tablespoons olive oil
- 1 tablespoon sake
- 2 tablespoons miso paste
- 2 tablespoons sugar
- 2 tablespoons mirin
- 2 tablespoons soy sauce

Instructions:
1. Preheat oven to 375°F (190°C).
2. Slice eggplants in half lengthwise, and cut into 3/4-inch (2 cm) thick slices.
3. Arrange eggplant onto a baking tray and brush with olive oil.
4. Bake in preheated oven for 30 minutes.
5. In a medium bowl, mix together the sake, miso paste, sugar, mirin, and soy sauce.
6. Brush this mixture on top of the eggplant slices.
7. Bake in preheated oven for 10 more minutes.

Nutrition information: Per serving- Calories: 328, Fat: 17 g, Saturated Fat: 2.5 g, Sodium: 1,086 mg, Carbohydrates: 38 g, Fiber: 13 g, Protein: 5.5 g

72. Korean Spicy Seafood Stew (Jjamppong)

Korean Spicy Seafood Stew (Jjamppong) is a flavorful and spicy stew made with seafood, vegetables, noodles, and a savory and spicy broth. It

is a popular dish in Korean restaurants and is sure to be a hit in any home.
Serving: 8
Preparation time: 10 minutes
Ready time: 40 minutes

Ingredients:
- 1 lb mussels
- 1 lb shrimp
- ½ lb squid
- 8 oz. udon or ramen noodles
- 4 cloves garlic, minced
- 2 green onions, sliced
- 4 carrots, sliced
- 2 celery stalks, sliced
- 1 red bell pepper, sliced
- 1 small onion, sliced
- 1 pack anchovy-kelp stock
- 2 tablespoons gochujang (Korean chili paste)
- 2 tablespoons vegetable oil
- 2 tablespoons soy sauce
- 2 tablespoons sesame oil
- 1 tablespoon mirin
- Salt and pepper to taste

Instructions:
1. Heat 2 tablespoons of vegetable oil in a large pot over medium-high heat.
2. Add garlic, green onions, carrots, celery, bell pepper, and onion to the pot. Stir-fry until vegetables are tender, about 5 minutes.
3. Add the anchovy-kelp stock, gochujang, soy sauce, sesame oil, and mirin to the pot. Stir to combine the Ingredients and let the mixture cook for about 5 minutes.
4. Add the mussels, shrimp, and squid to the pot and stir to combine the Ingredients. Let the mixture cook for about 10 minutes.
5. Add the udon noodles to the pot and stir until the noodles are cooked through, about 5 minutes.
6. Season with salt and pepper to taste.
7. Serve the stew in a bowl and enjoy!

Nutrition information:
Calories: 392, Total Fat: 13g, Saturated Fat: 2g, Cholesterol: 111mg, Sodium: 1110mg, Total Carbohydrate: 28g, Dietary Fiber: 4g, Total Sugars: 6g, Protein: 36g

73. Singaporean Satay Bee Hoon

Singaporean Satay Bee Hoon is a classic Singaporean dish made of stir-fried rice vermicelli and seafood in a flavorful peanut-coconut sauce.
Serving: 4 people
Preparation Time: 15 minutes
Ready Time: 25 minutes

Ingredients:
- 2 tablespoons oil
- 1 onion, sliced
- 4 cloves garlic, minced
- 2 tablespoons curry powder
- 1 tablespoon soy sauce
- 2 tablespoons peanut butter
- 1 cup coconut milk
- 1 pound seafood (shrimp, squid, crabmeat, etc.), cleaned and cut into bite-sized pieces
- 2 cups cooked bean sprouts
- 2 cups cooked rice vermicelli
- 4 tablespoons toasted peanuts

Instructions:
1. Heat the oil in a wok over medium-high heat.
2. Add the onion and garlic and cook until softened, about 3 minutes.
3. Add the curry powder, soy sauce, peanut butter, and coconut milk and stir to combine.
4. Add the seafood and stir to combine. Cook until the seafood is just cooked through, about 5 minutes.
5. Add the cooked bean sprouts and cooked rice vermicelli and stir to combine. Cook for 2 minutes.
6. Add the toasted peanuts and stir to combine.
7. Serve hot.

Nutrition information: Per serving - 390 calories, 21g fat, 5g saturated fat, 0g trans fat, 52g cholesterol, 1290mg sodium, 28g carbohydrates, 7g fiber, 11g sugar, 24g protein, 8% Vitamin A, 6% Vitamin C, 20% Calcium, and 10% Iron.

74. Thai Yellow Curry with Chicken

This Thai Yellow Curry with Chicken is full of flavorful, fragrant, and comforting Ingredients. Serve it over a bed of cooked jasmine rice for a delicious and easy dinner.
Serving: Serves 4
Preparation time: 30 minutes
Ready Time: 45 minutes

Ingredients:
- 2 tablespoons vegetable oil
- 1 large onion, chopped
- 2-3 cloves garlic, minced
- 2-3 tablespoons yellow curry paste
- 2 tablespoons brown sugar
- 1 teaspoon salt
- 2 tablespoons tamarind paste
- 1 (13.5 oz) can coconut milk
- 2 teaspoons fish sauce
- 2 tablespoons fresh lime juice
- 2 boneless, skinless chicken breasts, cut into cubes
- 1 red bell pepper, chopped
- 1 carrot, thinly sliced
- 1/2 cup fresh basil leaves, chopped
- Cooked jasmine rice, for Serving:

Instructions:
1. Heat the oil in a large skillet over medium-high heat.
2. Add the onion and cook, stirring occasionally, until softened and beginning to brown, about 5 minutes.
3. Add the garlic and curry paste and cook, stirring, for another minute.

4. Add the brown sugar, salt, tamarind paste, coconut milk, and fish sauce and bring to a simmer.
5. Add the chicken, bell pepper, and carrots and stir to combine.
6. Simmer until the chicken is cooked through and the vegetables are tender, about 10 minutes.
7. Stir in the fresh lime juice and basil.
8. Serve over cooked jasmine rice.

Nutrition information:
Calories: 292, Fat: 17g, Carbohydrates: 19g, Protein: 15g, Sodium: 843mg

75. Indian Malai Kofta

Indian Malai Kofta is a classic North Indian dish. It's a creamy, flavor-packed vegetarian entree of potato and paneer dumplings simmered in a rich gravy.
Serving: 4
Preparation time: 15 minutes
Ready time: 40 minutes

Ingredients:
- 2 large potatoes
- 100 grams paneer (cottage cheese), grated
- 2 tablespoons besan (gram flour)
- 2 tablespoons oil
- ½ teaspoon ground turmeric
- 2 tablespoons cilantro, finely chopped
- 6 – 7 cashew nuts, finely chopped
- 2 tablespoons raisins
- 1 teaspoon mango powder (amchoor)
- 2 tablespoons oil
- ½ teaspoon fennel seeds
- ½ teaspoon black cardamom seeds
- 1 teaspoon cumin seeds
- 1 medium onion, finely chopped
- 1 teaspoon ginger-garlic paste
- 1 teaspoon coriander powder
- 1 teaspoon garam masala

- 1 teaspoon red chilli powder
- ½ cup cream or malai
- Salt, to taste
- ½ teaspoon sugar
- 2 tablespoons chopped cilantro (for garnish)

Instructions:
1. Boil potatoes until tender, peel and mash. Add grated paneer to the potatoes, along with besan, turmeric, cilantro, cashew nuts and raisins. Mix together and make small balls out of the mixture.
2. Heat oil in a pan, fry the koftas until golden brown and keep aside.
3. In the same pan, add cumin, fennel and cardamom seeds and fry until they start to splutter.
4. Add onions and fry until golden brown. Add ginger-garlic paste, garam masala, red chilli powder, coriander powder and mango powder and fry for few minutes.
5. Add some water to the pan and bring to a boil. Add the cream, sugar and salt.
6. Add the koftas to the gravy and simmer for about 10-15 minutes.
7. Serve hot with a garnish of cilantro leaves.

Nutrition information: Calories: 250 kcal, Total Fat: 17 g, Saturated Fat: 6 g, Cholesterol: 25 mg, Sodium: 300 mg, Total Carbohydrate: 18 g, Dietary Fiber: 2 g, Protein: 6 g.

76. Malaysian Curry Chicken Bun

Malaysian Curry Chicken Bun is a delicious treat made with warm and spicy Malaysian curry chicken served inside a soft, grilled bun. It's sure to tantalize your tastebuds with its flavorful combination of Ingredients!
Serving: 4
Preparation Time: 10 minutes
Ready Time: 30 minutes

Ingredients:
- 2 tablespoons of oil
- 8 boneless, skinless chicken thighs, cut into cubes
- 2 tablespoons of Malaysian curry powder

- 2 tablespoons of dark soy sauce
- 1/2 cup of coconut milk
- 1 red onion, finely chopped
- 4 buns, split and lightly toasted

Instructions:
1. Heat the oil in a large frying pan over medium heat.
2. Add the chicken cubes and cook until golden brown, about 10 minutes.
3. Add the curry powder, dark soy sauce, and coconut milk and stir to combine.
4. Add the chopped onion and cook until the chicken is cooked through, about 10 more minutes.
5. Place the cooked chicken in the buns and serve.

Nutrition information:
Calories: 484, Protein: 25 g, Total Fat: 28 g, Saturated Fat: 9.3 g, Carbohydrates: 28 g, Fiber: 2 g, Sugar: 4 g, Sodium: 970 mg.

77. Vietnamese Coconut Curry Chicken

Vietnamese Coconut Curry Chicken is a delicious yet simple one-pot dish featuring chicken, coconut milk, curry powder, and vegetables. This flavorful dish is sure to please the whole family!
Serving: 4
Preparation Time: 10 minutes
Ready Time: 25 minutes

Ingredients:
- 2 tablespoons olive oil
- 1 large onion, diced
- 2 cloves garlic, minced
- 2 tablespoons Thai red curry paste
- 1 teaspoon ground ginger
- 2 boneless, skinless chicken breasts, cut into bite-sized pieces
- 1 can (14 ounces) coconut milk
- 1 can (14 ounces) diced tomatoes
- 2 tablespoons fish sauce

- 1 tablespoon brown sugar
- 1/2 teaspoon salt
- 1/2 teaspoon freshly ground black pepper
- 2 red bell peppers, sliced
- 2 cups snow peas
- 2 cups cooked white rice, for Serving:

Instructions:
1. Heat the oil in a large saucepan over medium heat. Add the onion and garlic and cook for 5 minutes, until the vegetables are tender.
2. Add the curry paste, ginger, and chicken pieces and cook for 2 minutes.
3. Add the coconut milk, tomatoes, fish sauce, brown sugar, salt, and pepper. Bring to a simmer and cook for 10 minutes, stirring occasionally.
4. Add the bell peppers and snow peas and cook for an additional 5 minutes, until the vegetables are tender.
5. Serve over cooked white rice, if desired.

Nutrition information: Calories: 327; Total Fat: 17g; Saturated Fat: 12g; Cholesterol: 43mg; Sodium: 816mg; Carbohydrates: 18g; Fiber: 4g; Sugar: 6g; Protein: 18g.

78. Indonesian Sayur Asem (Tamarind Vegetable Soup)

Indonesian Sayur Asem is a flavorful, slightly sweet and sour, vegan soup made of tamarind, vegetables and spices.
Serving – 4 servings
Preparation Time – 15 minutes
Ready Time – 45 minutes

Ingredients:
2 ounces tamarind paste
4 cups vegetable stock
1/2 can light coconut milk
1 tablespoon vegetable or coconut oil
1 onion, diced
3 cloves garlic, minced

2 carrots, sliced
2 potatoes, diced
1 teaspoon palm sugar or brown sugar
salt, to taste
1/2 red bell pepper, diced
1 tomato, cubed
1 tablespoon galangal grated
1 tablespoon lemongrass paste

Instructions:
1. In a pot, soak tamarind paste in 2 cups of boiling water for 10 minutes. Use a fork to mash tamarind in a pot until it breaks down into a paste.
2. Add vegetable stock, coconut milk, and oil to the pot. Bring the mixture to a boil, then reduce to a simmer.
3. Add onion, garlic, carrots, potatoes, palm sugar, and salt. Cook at a low simmer until potatoes are tender, about 25 minutes.
4. Add bell pepper, tomato, galangal, and lemongrass paste. Simmer for an additional 15 minutes.
5. Taste and adjust seasoning if necessary. Serve hot with steamed jasmine rice.

Nutrition information –
Calories: 122
Total Fat: 2.8g
Saturated Fat: 2.3g
Carbohydrates: 20.1g
Fiber: 3.2g
Protein: 2.9g

79. Thai Massaman Curry with Tofu

Enjoy the fragrant aroma of Thailand in this classic Thai Massaman Curry with Tofu. This vegan version uses coconut milk in place of the traditional beef or chicken, and pairs deliciously with all types of white and brown rice.
Serving: 4
Preparation Time: 10 minutes

Ready Time: 30 minutes

Ingredients:
- 14 ounces extra-firm tofu, pressing juice and cutting into cubes
- 2 tablespoons coconut oil or vegetable oil
- 1 yellow onion, finely diced
- 2 tablespoons Thai Massaman Curry Paste
- 1 can (14 ounce) coconut milk, full-fat or low-fat
- 2 tablespoons raw sugar or coconut sugar
- 2 tablespoons tamari or soy sauce
- 1 tablespoon freshly grated ginger
- 2 teaspoons chili-garlic paste
- 1 red bell pepper, cut into thin slices
- 1 tablespoon lime juice
- 2 tablespoons chopped fresh cilantro

Instructions:
1. Heat the oil in a large skillet over medium heat. Add the onions and sauté until golden brown, about 5 minutes.
2. Add the curry paste and cook until fragrant, about 2 minutes.
3. Add the coconut milk and stir to combine.
4. Add the sugar, tamari, ginger, and chili garlic paste and bring to a simmer.
5. Add the tofu cubes, bell pepper slices, and lime juice and simmer for 10 minutes.
6. Serve hot, topped with fresh cilantro.

Nutrition information: Serving Size: 1/4 recipe | Calories: 425 | Total Fat: 29 g | Total Carbohydrates: 33 g | Protein: 16 g | Fiber: 5 g | Sugar: 13 g

80. Japanese Yakisoba

Japanese Yakisoba is a popular Japanese noodle dish. It is made with a variety of Ingredients such as meats, vegetables, and yakisoba noodles. This dish is savory and delicious and a great addition to any meal.
Serving: 4
Preparation time: 20 minutes

Ready time: 40 minutes

Ingredients:
- 2 tablespoons vegetable oil
- 2 cloves garlic, minced
- 1 onion, chopped
- 1 carrot, julienned
- 1 bell pepper, julienned
- 1 1/2 cups sliced cabbage
- 1/2 pound ground beef
- 2 cups push yakisoba noodles
- 4 tablespoons yakisoba sauce
- 4 tablespoons Worcestershire sauce
- 1/2 teaspoon dried oregano
- Salt and pepper to taste

Instructions:
1. Heat the oil in a large skillet over medium-high heat. Add the garlic and onion, and cook for 2 minutes until the garlic is fragrant.
2. Add the carrot, bell pepper, and cabbage, and cook for 3 minutes until the vegetables begin to soften.
3. Push the vegetables to one side of the skillet and add the ground beef. Cook for 5 minutes, stirring occasionally, until the beef is cooked through.
4. Add the noodles and stir everything together. Pour the yakisoba sauce, Worcestershire sauce, and oregano over the noodles and stir.
5. Cook for 5 minutes until the noodles are cooked through, and season with salt and pepper.
6. Serve the yakisoba hot.

Nutrition information:
Serving Size: 1/4
Calories: 340
Total Fat: 13g
Saturated Fat: 5g
Cholesterol: 48mg
Sodium: 1048mg
Total Carbohydrates: 32g
Dietary Fiber: 3g
Sugars: 6g

Protein: 18g

81. Korean Jjajangmyeon

Korean Jjajangmyeon is a popular Korean noodle dish made with a salty black bean sauce. Serve it with a variety of toppings for a delicious and comforting meal!
Serving: 4
Preparation Time: 10 minutes
Ready Time: 20 minutes

Ingredients:
7 ounces jjajang (black bean) paste
2 tablespoons vegetable oil
2 cloves garlic, minced
1 small onion, diced
1 carrot, diced
3 ounces zucchini, diced
7 ounces pork belly, diced
5 cups chicken broth
12 ounces fresh noodles
Optional Toppings:
Chopped peanuts
Boiled egg
Green onions

Instructions:
1. Heat oil in a large pot over medium heat. Add garlic, onion, carrot, zucchini, and pork belly and cook for 5 minutes.
2. Add jjajang paste and cook for 3 minutes, stirring constantly.
3. Pour in chicken broth and bring to a boil.
4. Add fresh noodles and cook for 8-10 minutes, stirring occasionally.
5. Serve with optional toppings.

Nutrition information: (per serving)
Calories: 760
Fat: 44g
Carbohydrates: 53g

Protein: 37g
Sugar: 9g
Sodium: 1412mg

82. Singaporean Bak Kut Teh

Bak Kut Teh is a Chinese-style pork rib soup, originating from Singapore. It is fragrant, flavorful and can be enjoyed with a variety of traditional Ingredients such as mushrooms, tofu, and salted vegetables.
Serving: 4
Preparation Time: 10 minutes
Ready Time: 1 hour

Ingredients:
- 2 lbs pork ribs
- 5 cloves garlic, minced
- 6 dried shiitake mushrooms
- 2 tablespoons dark soy sauce
- 2 tablespoons light soy sauce
- 2 tablespoons oyster sauce
- 2 teaspoons sugar
- 1 cup chicken broth
- 2 teaspoons white pepper
- 1 teaspoon five-spice powder
- ¼ cup dried anchovies
- 3 tablespoons Chinese wolfberries

Instructions:
1. Soak the shiitake mushrooms in hot water for at least 15 minutes.
2. Add the pork ribs, garlic, and shiitake mushrooms to a large pot and cover with 8 cups of water. Bring the mixture to a boil, then reduce the heat and simmer for 45 minutes.
3. Add the dark soy sauce, light soy sauce, oyster sauce, sugar, chicken broth, white pepper, five-spice, anchovies, and wolfberries. Simmer for 15 minutes.
4. Serve hot with cooked rice.

Nutrition information: Per serving (without rice): Calories: 290, Fat: 11g, Saturated fat: 3g, Sodium: 626mg, Carbohydrates: 8g, Fiber: 2g, Sugar: 2g, Protein: 33g

83. Thai Green Curry with Beef

Thai Green Curry with Beef is a flavorful twist on the classic Thai curry dish. It combines savory beef with aromatic herbs and spices in a creamy coconut milk base for a delicious and comforting meal.
Serving: 4-6 people
Preparation Time: 10 minutes
Ready Time: 35 minutes

Ingredients:
- 1 lb beef sirloin, sliced into thin strips
- 1 large onion, diced
- 2 cloves garlic, minced
- 2 tablespoons Thai green curry paste
- 1 cup coconut milk
- 2 tablespoons fish sauce
- 1 tablespoon brown sugar
- 1 tablespoon freshly grated ginger
- 1 teaspoon ground coriander
- 1 teaspoon ground cumin
- 2 tablespoons vegetable oil
- 2 tablespoons chopped fresh basil
- 2 tablespoons chopped fresh cilantro

Instructions:
1. Heat oil in a large skillet over medium-high heat.
2. Add the beef strips and cook until lightly browned, about 5 minutes.
3. Reduce heat to medium and add the onion. Cook until softened, about 5 minutes.
4. Add the garlic and curry paste and cook, stirring, for 1 minute.
5. Add the coconut milk, fish sauce, brown sugar, ginger, coriander, and cumin. Simmer for 10 minutes.
6. Stir in the basil and cilantro and cook for an additional 5 minutes.
7. Serve over jasmine rice.

Nutrition information:
Calories: 320, Total Fat: 22g, Saturated Fat: 14g, Cholesterol: 50mg, Sodium: 600mg, Carbohydrates: 18g, Fiber: 3g, Protein: 17g

84. Indian Chicken Biryani

Indian Chicken Biryani is a favorite dish among South Asian countries. It is a flavorful, fragrant, and hearty one-pot meal with succulent pieces of chicken cooked in aromatic spices.
Serving: Serves 4
Preparation time: 15 minutes
Ready time: 1 hour 15 minutes

Ingredients:
- 2 to 3 lbs chicken, cut into small pieces
- 3 cups basmati rice
- 2 medium onions, finely sliced
- 3-4 cloves garlic, minced
- 2 tablespoons ginger-garlic paste
- 2 teaspoons cumin seeds
- 2 cinnamon sticks
- 1 bay leaf
- 2 tablespoons turmeric powder
- 1 teaspoon red chili powder
- 2 tablespoons coriander powder
- 2 tablespoons garam masala
- 2 tablespoons cilantro, chopped
- 2 tablespoons mint, chopped
- 1 cup yogurt, whisked
- 1/2 cup ghee or clarified butter
- 2 tablespoons vegetable oil
- Salt to taste
- 1 teaspoon sugar
- 2-3 cups water

Instructions:

1. Combine chicken pieces, yogurt, 1 tablespoon of the ginger-garlic paste, 1 teaspoon red chili powder, 1 tablespoon of coriander powder, 1 teaspoon turmeric powder, 1 teaspoon salt and 1 teaspoon sugar in a large bowl. Refrigerate for at least 30 minutes.
2. Heat ghee and oil in a large pot, and add cumin seeds, cinnamon sticks, bay leaf, and the remaining ginger-garlic paste. Sauté for 1 minute.
3. Add the sliced onion and sauté until lightly browned.
4. Add the marinated chicken and stir fry for 5 minutes.
5. Add garam masala, cilantro, and mint and continue to stir fry for 5 minutes.
6. Add basmati rice, mix well, and season with salt according to taste.
7. Add 2 to 3 cups of water, depending on the desired consistency, cover the pot and cook the biryani on low-medium heat until the chicken is cooked through, about 10-15 minutes.
8. Garnish with cilantro and mint and serve hot.

Nutrition information:
Calories: 680, Protein: 34g, Fat: 25g, Sodium: 580mg, Carbohydrates: 68g, Fiber: 6g, Sugars: 8g

85. Malaysian Assam Laksa

Malaysian Assam Laksa is an immensely popular noodle soup from Malaysia. The soup has a delightful balance of sweet, savory, spicy and tangy flavors that make it full of flavor and rich in texture. Servings: 4-6 Preparation Time: 20 minutes Ready Time:25 minutes

Ingredients:
- 2 cups tamarind water
- 2 cups water
- ¼ cup fish sauce
- 2 teaspoons chili paste
- 3 tablespoons sugar
- 1 tablespoon chopped garlic
- 2 teaspoons ground coriander
- ½ teaspoon shrimp paste
- 1 teaspoon sesame oil
- 2 cups cooked, shredded chicken

- 1 pound fresh noodles
- 1 ½ cups bean sprouts
- 1 large cucumber, peeled, seeded and sliced
- ½ cup boiled peanuts

Instructions:
1. In a medium saucepan, combine tamarind water, water, fish sauce, chili paste, sugar, garlic, coriander and shrimp paste. Bring to a boil and cook for 10 minutes.
2. Add the sesame oil, chicken, cooked noodles, bean sprouts and cucumber. Stir to combine and cook for an additional 3-5 minutes.
3. Divide the ingredients among 4-6 serving bowls and top with boiled peanuts.

Nutrition information: Per serving, Malaysian Assam Laksa contains approximately 500 calories, 15.1g fat, 35.2g carbohydrates, 6.8g fiber, 25.7g protein and 1550mg sodium.

86. Vietnamese Clay Pot Chicken

Vietnamese Clay Pot Chicken is an easy and flavorful dinner that comes together quickly. Slices of chicken are simmered in a savory and slightly sweet sauce, and accompanied by crunchy vegetables.

Serving
Serves 4
Preparation time
10 minutes
Ready time
50 minutes

Ingredients:
- 1 1/2 pounds of boneless skinless chicken thighs
- 1/3 cup oyster sauce
- 2 tablespoons soy sauce
- 2 tablespoons sugar
- 2 tablespoons fish sauce
- 2 cloves of garlic, minced
- 1 teaspoon fresh ginger, minced

- 2 tablespoons vegetable oil
- 2 Serrano chili peppers, sliced
- 1 red bell pepper, sliced
- 2 cups chicken broth
- 1/4 cup of cilantro, chopped
- 2 scallions, sliced

Instructions:
1. In a bowl, mix together the oyster sauce, soy sauce, sugar, and fish sauce, stirring until the sugar is dissolved.
2. Heat a clay pot over medium-high heat. Add in the vegetable oil, garlic, and ginger, stir-frying for 1 minute until fragrant.
3. Add in the chicken thighs and Serrano chili peppers, and stir-fry for a few minutes until the chicken starts to brown.
4. Add the red bell pepper and pour in the sauce, stirring to coat the chicken.
5. Add the chicken broth, cover, and reduce heat to low. Simmer for 30 minutes, stirring occasionally, until the chicken is cooked through.
6. Uncover the pot and turn the heat up to high. Simmer for a few minutes to reduce the sauce.
7. Top with cilantro and scallions before serving.

Nutrition information
Per Serving (1/4 of recipe): Calories 419; Fat 24.1g; Saturated Fat 9.3g; Cholesterol 137mg, Sodium 907mg; Protein 34.3g; Carbohydrates 16.1g; Fiber 2.1g; Sugar 11g

87. Indonesian Opor Ayam (Chicken in Coconut Milk)

Indonesian Opor Ayam is a traditional Indonesian dish, featuring chicken pieces cooked in flavorful coconut milk. The rich coconut sauce infuses the chicken with a unique flavor, making it the perfect meal for any occasion.

Serving:
4
Preparation time:
30 minutes

Ready time:
1 hour

Ingredients:
- 2 lbs chicken drumsticks or thighs, skin on
- 2 tablespoons vegetable oil
- 5 shallots, chopped
- 3 cloves garlic, chopped
- 2-3 bird's eye chilies, finely chopped
- 2 lemongrass stalks
- 6 kaffir lime leaves
- 2 salam leaves
- 2 tablespoons ground coriander
- ½ teaspoon ground cumin
- 1 teaspoon ground turmeric
- 1 teaspoon ground black pepper
- 2 cups coconut milk
- 2 tablespoons brown sugar
- 2 tablespoons tamarind paste
- 2 tablespoons fish sauce
- salt, to taste

Instructions:
1. Heat the oil in a large pot or Dutch oven over medium heat.
2. Add the shallots, garlic, and chilies and cook until fragrant, about 3 minutes.
3. Add the chicken and cook until lightly browned, about 5 minutes.
4. Add the lemongrass, kaffir lime leaves, salam leaves, coriander, cumin, turmeric, and black pepper and cook, stirring regularly, until the spices are fragrant, about 2 minutes.
5. Pour in the coconut milk, brown sugar, tamarind paste, and fish sauce. Stir to combine.
6. Bring the mixture to a boil, then reduce the heat and simmer for 45 minutes, or until the chicken is cooked through.
7. Taste and adjust seasoning if needed.
8. Serve hot over steamed rice.

Nutrition information:
Calories: 421, Total fat: 28g, Saturated fat: 20g, Cholesterol: 128mg, Sodium: 534mg, Carbohydrate: 12g, Fiber: 1g, Sugar: 5g, Protein: 28g

88. Thai Red Curry with Pork

This Thai Red Curry with Pork is a spicy, flavorful and aromatic dish that is full of traditional Thai flavors. Making a great main course for dinner, this dish is surprisingly easy to make and is sure to delight the entire family.

Serving: Serves 4
Preparation Time: 10 minutes
Ready Time: 30 minutes

Ingredients:
- 1 tablespoon vegetable oil
- 2 tablespoons Thai red curry paste
- 2 cloves garlic, minced
- 1 small onion, finely chopped
- 2 cups chicken broth
- 1 can coconut milk
- 1 tablespoon fish sauce
- 2 tablespoons light brown sugar
- 1 teaspoon lime zest
- ½ teaspoon salt
- 12 ounces pork tenderloin, cut into 1/2-inch cubes
- 2 red bell peppers, sliced
- 1 (8-ounce) can bamboo shoots
- 1/4 cup fresh basil leaves, chopped

Instructions:
1. Heat oil in a wok or large skillet over medium heat. Add curry paste, garlic and onion, and cook for 2 minutes.
2. Add broth, coconut milk, fish sauce, brown sugar, lime zest, and salt. Simmer for 10 minutes.
3. Add pork cubes, bell pepper slices and bamboo shoots. Simmer for 10 minutes.
4. Add basil leaves and cook for 1 minute. Serve over cooked white or brown rice.

Nutrition information: calories: 327; total fat: 18.7 g; saturated fat: 12.9 g; sodium: 953 mg; total carbohydrate: 17.8 g; dietary fiber: 3.9 g; sugars: 11.1 g; protein: 17.2 g.

89. Japanese Teriyaki Chicken

This recipe for Teriyaki Chicken is one of Japan's most popular dishes! Its smooth, sweet and savory sauce makes it the perfect accompaniment for any meal.
Serving: 4 servings
Preparation time: 10 minutes
Ready time: 35 minutes

Ingredients:
- 4 boneless chicken breasts
- 1/4 cup soy sauce
- 1/4 cup of honey
- 3 tablespoons of Mirin
- 1 teaspoon of grated ginger
- 2 cloves of garlic, minced
- 1 tablespoon of vegetable oil
- 2 tablespoons of sake or white wine

Instructions:
1. In a large bowl whisk together the soy sauce, honey, mirin, ginger, garlic, vegetable oil, and sake or white wine.
2. Add the chicken breasts to the marinade and let sit for 10 minutes.
3. Heat a skillet over medium-high heat.
4. Remove the chicken from the marinade and cook for 7-8 minutes on each side, or until the chicken is cooked through.
5. Once the chicken has finished cooking, add the remaining marinade to the skillet and cook for 5-6 minutes.
6. Once the sauce has thickened it's time to plate! Serve the chicken on a plate and top off with the sauce.

Nutrition information: 400 calories, 18 g fat, 5 g saturated fat, 70 mg cholesterol, 820 mg sodium, 22 g carbohydrates, 19 g protein.

90. Korean Gamjatang (Spicy Pork Bone Soup)

Korean Gamjatang is a comforting and spicy pork bone soup that is popular throughout Korea and served as a meal. It is a hearty and flavorful dish that is both nourishing and satisfying.
Serving: 4 Servings
Preparation time: 10 minutes
Ready time: 1 hour and 20 minutes

Ingredients:
-4 lbs pork neck bones
-8 dried red chili peppers
-10 garlic cloves, minced
-½ cup onion, sliced
-2 tbs gochugaru (Korean chili flakes)
-2 tbs soy sauce
-2 tbs fish sauce
-1 tbs black pepper
-4 green onions, thinly sliced
-1 tbs sesame oil
-4 potatoes, peeled and cubed
-1 small Korean radish, peeled and cubed

Instructions:
1. Rinse pork neck bones and set aside.
2. In a large pot, add dried red chili peppers and garlic cloves. Sauté until lightly browned.
3. Add onion slices and pork neck bones and cook for about 5 minutes.
4. Add gochugaru, soy sauce, fish sauce, black pepper, and enough water to cover the pork neck bones.
5. Bring to a boil, reduce heat and simmer for 45 minutes.
6. Add green onions, sesame oil, potatoes, and radish and cook for an additional 20 minutes or until the potatoes and radish are tender.
7. Serve with white rice and garnish with more green onions.

Nutrition information:
Calories: 358 kcal, Carbohydrates: 20 g, Protein: 24.3 g, Fat: 19.8 g, Saturated Fat: 6.5 g, Cholesterol: 73 mg, Sodium: 836 mg, Potassium: 956

mg, Fiber: 2.5 g, Sugar: 4.2 g, Vitamin A: 482 IU, Vitamin C: 35 mg, Calcium: 58 mg, Iron: 4 mg.

91. Singaporean Char Kway Teow

Singaporean Char Kway Teow is a delectable dish consisting of fried noodles with seafood, vegetables, and a variety of savory sauces. It is sure to tantalize your taste buds!
Serving: 4
Preparation Time: 15 minutes
Ready Time: 20 minutes

Ingredients:
- 1 package of kway teow (flat rice noodles)
- 2 tablespoons vegetable oil
- 1 onion, diced
- 2 cloves garlic, diced
- 4 shrimp, peeled & deveined
- 1 tablespoon soy sauce
- 1 teaspoon sugar
- 1/2 teaspoon chili paste
- 3 eggs, beaten
- 1/2 cup Chinese cabbage, shredded
- 1/2 carrot, diced
- 1/2 green bell pepper, diced
- 4 ounces bean sprouts
- 1/4 cup frozen peas
- 2 green onions, chopped
- 1 teaspoon sesame oil

Instructions:
1. Heat the oil in a large skillet or wok over medium-high heat. Add the onion and garlic, cook for 1-2 minutes.
2. Add the shrimp and cook until just done, about 3 minutes.
3. Add the soy sauce, sugar, and chili paste and stir fry for 1 minute.
4. Add the eggs and scramble until just done, about 1 minute.
5. Add the cabbage, carrot, bell pepper, bean sprouts, peas, and green onions and stir fry for 3 minutes.

6. Add the kway teow and sesame oil and stir fry for 4-5 minutes.
7. Serve the Char Kway Teow hot.

Nutrition information: Per Serving: Calories: 311, Total Fat: 7.6g, Cholesterol: 64.8mg, Sodium: 492.9mg, Carbohydrates: 45.7g, Fiber: 2.9g, Protein: 12.1g

92. Thai Pad See Ew

Thai Pad See Ew is a popular street food dish in Thailand, which consists of flat rice noodles stir-fried with eggs, Chinese broccoli, and a savory sauce.
Serving: 4
Preparation time: 15 minutes
Ready time: 25 minutes

Ingredients:
- 8 ounces wide, flat rice noodles
- 2 tablespoons vegetable oil
- 2 eggs, beaten
- 1/2 pound Chinese broccoli, chopped
- 2 cloves garlic minced
- 2 tablespoons dark soy sauce
- 2 tablespoons oyster sauce
- 2 tablespoons fish sauce
- 2 tablespoons white sugar
- 2 tablespoons water

Instructions:
1. Soak the rice noodles in warm water for 10 minutes until softened.
2. Heat the vegetable oil in a large wok over medium-high heat. Add the eggs and scramble until cooked through.
3. Add the Chinese broccoli and garlic and stir-fry for 1-2 minutes, or until the vegetables are softened.
4. Add the noodles and stir-fry for an additional 2-3 minutes, until the noodles are softened.

5. Add the dark soy sauce, oyster sauce, fish sauce, white sugar, and water. Stir-fry until all the Ingredients are combined and the noodles are cooked through.
6. Stir in the excess liquid from the noodles and cook for 1-2 minutes, or until the liquid is absorbed.

Nutrition information: Per serving: 439 calories; 19.7 g fat; 50.7 g carbohydrates; 18.2 g protein; 6.8 g fiber; 901 mg sodium.

93. Indian Egg Curry

Indian Egg Curry is an easy-to-make, flavorful curry dish that is sure to please. It is a great way to add protein to a vegetarian meal.
Serving: 4
Preparation time: 20 minutes
Ready time: 30 minutes

Ingredients:
- 6 eggs, hard boiled and peeled
- 2 tablespoons vegetable oil
- 1 onion, finely chopped
- 1 teaspoon fresh ginger, grated
- 2 cloves garlic, minced
- 3 tomatoes, finely chopped
- 2 tablespoons ground coriander
- 1 teaspoon ground cumin
- 1 teaspoon ground turmeric
- 1 teaspoon garam masala
- 1/2 teaspoon chili powder
- 1/2 teaspoon ground black pepper
- 1 cup water
- 1/4 cup heavy cream
- Salt to taste

Instructions:
1. Heat oil in a large saucepan over medium heat.
2. Add onion and cook until softened, about 3 minutes.
3. Add ginger and garlic and cook for 1 minute.

4. Add tomatoes, coriander, cumin, turmeric, garam masala, chili powder, black pepper, and water. Stir to combine.
5. Bring to a gentle boil, reduce heat to low, and simmer for 10 minutes.
6. Add the hard-boiled eggs and simmer for an additional 5 minutes.
7. Stir in the cream and simmer for another 2 minutes.
8. Taste and season with salt as needed.

Nutrition information:
Calories: 335, Total Fat: 24.3g, Saturated Fat: 8.1g, Cholesterol: 208mg, Sodium: 277mg, Carbohydrates: 14.3g, Fiber: 4.9g, Sugar: 7.2g, Protein: 16.2g

94. Malaysian Curry Mee

Malaysian Curry Mee is a comforting and hearty noodle soup that is cooked in rich and creamy coconut milk. Bursting with flavor, it is a popular dish among many Malaysians.
Serving: 4
Preparation time: 15 minutes
Ready time: 45 minutes

Ingredients:
- 2 tablespoons cooking oil
- 1 tablespoon red curry paste
- 1 stalk lemongrass, smashed
- 3 cloves garlic, minced
- 2 shallots, minced
- 2 Thai red chilies, diced
- 5 ounces boneless skinless chicken thighs, cubed
- 5 ounces firm tofu, cubed
- 4 cups chicken stock
- 2 tablespoons fish sauce
- 4 tablespoons soy sauce
- 1 tablespoon sugar
- 2 cups coconut milk
- 8 ounces egg noodles
- 2 tablespoons lime juice

Instructions:
1. Heat the oil in a large pot over medium-high heat.
2. Add the curry paste, lemongrass, garlic, shallots, and chilies and sauté for 2 minutes.
3. Add the chicken and tofu and cook for 5 minutes.
4. Add the chicken stock, fish sauce, soy sauce, sugar, and coconut milk and bring to a boil.
5. Add the noodles and reduce the heat to medium-low and simmer for 10 minutes.
6. Pour in the lime juice and remove from the heat.
7. Ladle the curry mee into bowls and serve hot.

Nutrition information:
Calories 332, Fat 16.8g, Cholesterol 46mg, Sodium 1209mg, Carbohydrates 32.4g, Protein 15.4g

95. Vietnamese Shrimp Pho

Vietnamese Shrimp Pho is a classic Vietnamese noodle soup dish. It is packed full of flavor and can easily be made at home!
Serving: 4 servings
Preparation time: 10 minutes
Ready time: 40 minutes

Ingredients:
- 2 tablespoons of vegetable oil
- 1 large onion, thinly sliced
- 2 cloves of garlic, minced
- 3 tablespoons of tomato paste
- 2 tablespoons of fish sauce
- 1.5 litres of chicken stock
- 2 teaspoons of sugar
- 1 teaspoon of freshly grated ginger
- 1 teaspoon of ground coriander
- 500g dried flat rice noodles
- 500g large green prawns, peeled and deveined
- 1 small red chilli, finely sliced
- 2 tablespoons of chopped fresh coriander leaves

- 2 limes, quartered

Instructions:
1. Heat the oil in a large saucepan over medium heat.
2. Add the onion and garlic. Cook until the onion is soft and golden.
3. Add the tomato paste, fish sauce, stock, sugar, ginger and ground coriander.
4. Bring to the boil, then reduce the heat to low and simmer for 30 minutes.
5. Meanwhile, cook the rice noodles according to packet instructions and set aside.
6. Add the prawns to the soup and cook for 3-4 minutes until just cooked through.
7. Taste and adjust the seasoning if necessary.
8. Divide the noodles among four bowls and add the soup.
9. Top with chilli, coriander leaves and lime.

Nutrition information: Per serving - Calories: 388, Total Fat: 10g, Saturated Fat: 2.5g, Cholesterol: 86mg, Sodium: 1759.2mg, Carbohydrates: 50.8g, Fiber: 2.9g, Sugar: 6.5g, Protein: 23.9g

96. Indonesian Sambal Goreng Udang (Spicy Stir-fried Shrimp)

Indonesian Sambal Goreng Udang is a delicious stir-fried shrimp dish that is well-loved all over the country. This flavorful and spicy dish is made with savory shrimp, garlic, shallots, ginger, red chili peppers, sugar and rice wine. It makes a savory accompaniment to plain boiled rice or fried noodles.
Serving: Serves 4
Preparation time: 15 minutes
Ready time: 30 minutes

Ingredients:
- 1 pound large shrimp, peeled and deveined
- 2 tablespoons vegetable oil
- 4 cloves garlic, minced
- 2 shallots, minced

- 2 tablespoons minced fresh ginger
- 4 red chili peppers, diced
- 1 teaspoon sugar
- 2 tablespoons Chinese rice wine

Instructions:
1. Heat oil in a large wok until hot, about 2 minutes.
2. Add garlic, shallots and ginger. Stir-fry for 1-2 minutes.
3. Add chili peppers and shrimp. Stir-fry until the shrimp turns pink, about 3 minutes.
4. Add sugar and rice wine. Stir-fry for an additional 1-2 minutes.
5. Serve.

Nutrition information
Per Serving: 485 calories; 25.3 g fat; 28.4 g carbohydrates; 38.6 g protein; 270 mg cholesterol; 1610 mg sodium.

97. Thai Yellow Curry with Seafood

This Thai Yellow Curry with Seafood is an intense flavor dish utilizing the sweetness of the coconut milk and the savory, pungent taste of the yellow curry paste and is sure to be an instant favorite.
Serving: 4
Preparation Time: 10 minutes
Ready Time: 20 minutes

Ingredients:
- 2 tablespoons yellow curry paste
- 2 tablespoons vegetable oil
- ½ cup coconut milk
- 1 pound shrimp, cleaned and deveined
- 1 cup green or red bell pepper, diced
- 1 teaspoon fish sauce
- 2 cloves garlic, crushed
- ¼ teaspoon salt
- 2 cups cooked Jasmine rice

Instructions:

1. Heat a large skillet over medium-high heat.
2. Add the curry paste and vegetable oil, stirring to combine.
3. Add the coconut milk and reduce the heat to low. Simmer for about 4 minutes.
4. Add the shrimp, bell peppers, fish sauce, garlic, and salt. Simmer for another 6 minutes.
5. Serve the Thai yellow curry with seafood over cooked Jasmine rice.

Nutrition information: per serving: Calories: 406 • Fat: 15.2g • Saturated Fat: 12.1g • Cholesterol: 191mg • Sodium: 1098mg • Carbohydrate: 41.4g • Fiber: 2.7g • Protein: 24.1g

98. Japanese Tempura

Enjoy the simplest form of Japanese cuisine with this delicious Japanese Tempura recipe. This traditional deep-fried dish is made with a light batter and various vegetables and seafood. Crispy on the outside but perfectly tender on the inside, it will be the star of the dinner table.
Serving: 4-6
Preparation Time: 20 minutes
Ready Time: 10 minutes

Ingredients:
-1 lb vegetables of your choice such as broccoli, mushrooms, green beans, onions, zucchini, sweet potatoes, etc.
-1 lb seafood of your choice such as shrimp, scallops, fish slices, etc.
-1 ½ cup all-purpose flour
-1 ½ cup cold water
-2 tsp baking soda
-⅔ cup cornstarch
-Vegetable oil, for deep-frying

Instructions:
1. Cut vegetables into large chunks.
2. Peel and devein shrimp, and then cut into 1-inch lengths.
3. In a medium bowl, whisk together the flour, water, baking soda and cornstarch until a smooth batter is formed.
4. Heat the oil in a large deep skillet to 350°F.

5. Dip the vegetables and seafood into the batter and carefully add them to the hot oil. Fry for 2-3 minutes or until golden brown.
6. Remove the tempura from the oil with a slotted spoon and place on paper towels to drain. Serve immediately.

Nutrition information:
Calories: 300, Fat: 13g, Sodium: 254mg, Carbs: 29g, Protein: 16g

99. Korean Doenjang Jjigae (Fermented Soybean Paste Stew)

Doenjang jjigae, also known as Korean fermented soybean paste stew, is a popular Korean dish. It is made with a wide variety of Ingredients including doenjang (fermented soybean paste), vegetables, anchovy broth, and occasionally seafood. It is commonly served with steamed white rice and other banchan dishes.
Serving: 4-6 people
Preparation Time: 15 minutes
Ready Time: 45 minutes

Ingredients:
- 5 tablespoons of doenjang (fermented soybean paste)
- 4 cups of anchovy broth
- 2 cloves of garlic, minced
- 2 tablespoons of gochujang (Korean hot pepper paste)
- 1 onion, diced
- 1 zucchini, cut into bite-size pieces
- 1 medium potato, cut into bite-size pieces
- Optional: 4 ounces of seafood, such as shrimp, squid, and clams

Instructions:
1. Heat a pot over medium-high heat and add the doenjang. Stir until the paste is melted and fragrant, about 2 minutes.
2. Add the anchovy broth and garlic and stir to combine. Bring the liquid to a boil.
3. Once boiling, reduce the heat to medium-low and add the gochujang, onion, zucchini, and potato. Stir to combine.
4. Simmer for 30 minutes, stirring occasionally.

5. If using, add the seafood and simmer for an additional 5-10 minutes, or until the seafood is cooked through.
6. Serve the stew with steamed white rice and other banchan dishes. Enjoy!

Nutrition information (per serving): Calories: 176, Fat: 9g, Cholesterol: 21mg, Sodium: 146mg, Carbohydrates: 13g, Protein: 10g.

100. Malaysian Beef Curry

Malaysian Beef Curry is an exotic and flavorful curry that is cooked with beef, potatoes, and a variety of spices that combine to create an incredible dish of comfort food.
Serving: 4
Preparation time: 30 minutes
Ready time: 1 hour

Ingredients:
- 2 tbsp vegetable oil
- 2 lbs beef stew meat, cut into 1-inch cubes
- 1 large onion, diced
- 3 cloves garlic, minced
- 1 tbsp fresh ginger, minced
- 2 tsp ground cumin
- 2 tsp ground coriander
- 2 tsp turmeric
- 2 tsp ground cardamom
- 1 tbsp curry powder
- 2 large potatoes, cubed
- 1 (14.5 oz) can diced tomatoes
- 1/2 cup beef broth
- 1/2 cup coconut milk

Instructions:
1. Heat the oil in a large skillet over medium-high heat.
2. Add the beef and cook until lightly browned.
3. Add the onion, garlic, and ginger and cook until softened.

4. Add the cumin, coriander, turmeric, cardamom, and curry powder and stir to combine.
5. Add the potatoes, tomatoes, beef broth, and coconut milk and stir to combine.
6. Bring to a boil, reduce heat, and simmer, covered, for 30 minutes.
7. Uncover and simmer until the sauce is thickened and the beef and potatoes are tender.

Nutrition information: Calories: 427, Fat: 23g, Carbohydrates: 27g, Protein: 28g, Fiber: 4g, Sodium: 389mg

CONCLUSION

Curry Craze: Your Ultimate Guide to 100 Flavorful Recipes provides a unique opportunity to explore a diverse array of flavor profiles from around the world. For both the seasoned cook and the novice alike, this book is the perfect companion for creating easy, delicious dishes that will be sure to impress. From delectable starters like shrimp and paneer pakoras to vegetarian-friendly delights like Keralan vegetable curry, this book provides all of the recipes, tips, tricks, and techniques to achieve mind-blowing meal results.

The 100 flavorful recipes featured in Curry Craze are geared toward any home cook looking to expand beyond their current comfort zone. With spice profiles ranging from mild to wild, the book is sure to offer something for everyone regardless of their heat preference. With sections on vegan, gluten-free, one-pot, and family-friendly dishes, there are plenty of options for those looking to impress and also minimize their time spent in the kitchen.

As well as offering recipes, Curry Craze also provides a wealth of background information on ingredients and their uses, as well as an exhaustive glossary for unfamiliar terms. This book imparts the knowledge and understanding a cook needs to tackle any dish on their own without having to make multiple trips to the grocery store.

Curry Craze is not only a great reference for recipes, but can also act as a guide to familiarizing readers with the exciting flavors offered by authentic Indian cuisine. Even if you're a novice to the art of cooking, this book can still help you quickly become adept in cooking with spices and their many nuances. No matter what level of expertise you're at, following the instructions in Curry Craze can open up an entirely new realm of flavors for you to explore.

From appetizers to entrees to sweet treats, Curry Craze is the ultimate guide to crafting flavorful dishes for every occasion. After trying out the recipes in this book, you will quickly become an expert in crafting tantalizing meals. So, for an exciting and adventurous journey through the world of Indian cuisine, you can't do much better than Curry Craze: Your Ultimate Guide to 100 Flavorful Recipes.

Printed in Great Britain
by Amazon